APE FEAR TECHNICAL INSTITUTE

NORTH CAROLINA
STATE BOARD OF EDUCATION
DEPT. OF COMMUNITY COLLEGES
LIBRARIES

D0848589

# THE LONGSHOREMEN

Southwold beach about 1905. At that time nearly every coastal town and village had its own fleet of small craft.

# THE
# LONGSHOREMEN

Roy Clark

DAVID & CHARLES

NEWTON ABBOT    LONDON

NORTH POMFRET (VT)    VANCOUVER

ISBN 0 7153 6484 7

© Roy Clark 1974

FOR MARGARET

All rights reserved No part of this publication
may be reproduced  stored in a retrieval system
or transmitted  in any form or by any means
electronic  mechanical  photocopying  recording
or otherwise  without the prior  permission of
David & Charles (Holdings) Limited

Set in 11 on 13pt Plantin
and printed in Great Britain
by W J Holman Limited  Dawlish
for David & Charles (Holdings) Limited
South Devon House  Newton Abbot  Devon


Published in the United States of America
by David & Charles Inc  North Pomfret  Vermont 05053  USA


Published in Canada
by Douglas David & Charles Limited  3645 McKechnie Drive
West Vancouver BC

# Contents

# List of Illustrations

IN TEXT

# CHAPTER ONE

# Years Ago

'Come on, young 'un, if yew've a mind t' go fishin',' said the skipper of Y.H.62., directing an amiable wink at his crew, two sturdy longshoremen like himself, 'yew've bin worritin' me for t' take yew I doan't know how long, so now's yer chance,' and seizing me in his massive arms, lifted me over the side of the boat, standing ready for launching at the water's edge, and plonked me down on the for'ard thwart, well out of the way. 'An' dew yew stay jest where yew are, now,' he added, 'an' doan't move till I tell 'e tew.'

Move! I couldn't have moved to save my life. I was too thrilled, too bursting with excitement, to do more than sit perfectly still, both hands beside me holding on to the thwart, wondering just how I should feel when the boat was pushed off and we began bounding through the waves.

I suppose I was about ten years old then and although I'd paddled and splashed about in the sea, even tried to swim a stroke or two, never before had I been in a boat; this was to be my first voyage! No wonder I was so excited!

The skipper was standing by the stern with one or two others who'd come along to give us a shove off. All wore white thigh-boots, black oilskins, caps and a red neckerchief round their throats. I heard the skipper being chaffed about 'th' manful-lookin' crew' he was taking with him but he only nodded good-humouredly as he made sure the rudder and tiller were lying handy and looked to see the yard and sail were clear for hoisting. Then he set his shoulder to the boat's stern, the others close beside him, and watched for a bigger wave to come in and float her forepart. It soon arrived, frothing and gurgling round the stem, when he sang out, 'All on yer, now! H-e-a-v-e!'

I felt the bow lift, hesitate a second, then the whole boat slid forward, faster and faster, till with a scrambling jump the skipper pulled himself in over the quarter. The crew plied their oars vigorously keeping her head on to the waves though for the first few strokes they were scraping the blades on the sandy bottom. Soon there was deep water under us and in a few minutes after a strong, but unhurried, pull, we got an offing of fifty yards or more.

Then I heard the skipper say, quite casually, 'Thet'll about dew us', as he took up the rudder, carefully married gudgeons and pintles, and slid it into position. The crew unshipped their oars and stowed them across the two centre thwarts. 'Best have th' boy Roy aft here,' he added, 'so's I cen keep an eye on 'im. Give 'im a hand, yew tew,' and with great care I was jockeyed round the pile of herring nets and into the sternsheets.

'An' now let's giv' 'er some cloth,' were his next words, which, if it were possible, made me even more excited, because I knew the expression 'to give her some cloth' meant getting up the sail. So I watched, fascinated, as one of the crew took the hook at the end of the halliard, slipped it through an eye on the yard, then joined his companion to haul the spread of black, heavy canvas into the sky. The tack was already secured to the stem and all that remained was for the skipper to ship the tiller, which he'd kept ready under his feet, into the rudder, gather in the slack of the sheet, and we were away. There was a light but steady breeze, partly off the land, out of the south-west, a fine quartering wind to carry us over the young flood tide till we had Winterton Ness abeam, a mile or so to the north. Somewhere about there, I knew, the sail would some down, one of the crew would man both oars while the other and the skipper shot the nets. I'd watched it happen so many times from the beach but never in my wildest dreams did I ever think that one day I should be out there in a boat myself, going fishing as one of the crew.

I remember clearly how at first I kept looking at the shore and thinking how different everything seemed. We were only out a hundred yards but familiar landmarks like bushes, distant farm houses and the far away church tower took on a new perspective. The skipper, arm crooked round the tiller, cupped his hands, struck a match and re-lit his pipe. 'Well, young 'un,' he enquired, 'how's it feel to be a fisherman, eh?' One of the crew, busy attaching a float to the first net ready for shooting, remarked with a grin, 'Soon know whether 'e be a Jonah or no, won't we?' 'What's a Jonah?' I asked, rather timidly. They all laughed and I felt foolish. The skipper ruffled my hair with his free hand then patted my head reassuringly, explaining that anyone who brought bad luck was called a Jonah, but that he didn't think I was one.

And as things turned out, he was right. We put the nets over as soon as we'd got to Winterton Ness when the tide we'd been sailing against began carrying us back again. Once or twice we 'looked on', that is, pulled part of the first net on board, and found quite a few fish. The skipper removed about a dozen, let the net go again, and strung a piece of yarn through their gills and mouth. 'Them's fer yer mother t' fry fer breakfast,' said the skipper handing them to me, adding, 'an now, seein' as how it's gettin' dark, I'm agoin' to put yew ashore right where we started from.'

Needless to say I was disappointed; I wanted so much to stay till the flood finished and the nets were hauled in to see how big the catch was. But that wouldn't happen for another three or four hours when I ought to be tucked up and fast asleep. 'Never mind,' said the skipper kindly, obviously seeing my glum face, 'there's always another day termorrer, yew cen come agen along o' us.' What joyful words they were to my young ears! I could actually go again! Now I didn't mind hopping ashore as the boat was pulled in to the beach and clutching my string of herrings, watched contentedly as Y.H.62. returned to her nets to continue drifting up the coast into the gathering dusk.

There was no prouder lad that night as I handed the herrings to my mother but one thing did worry me a bit; suppose they only got a small catch? They'd reckon I was a Jonah and probably wouldn't let me go with them any more. As things turned out I needn't have worried. Next morning I saw Y.H.62. come sailing along close inshore and as we all lent a hand shortly afterwards to haul her up the beach I learned that she'd taken so many fish that

the skipper decided to sail into Great Yarmouth harbour and land
them at the herring quay. The three of them looked tired but
pretty well pleased with their night's work, then seeing me with a
broad grin on my face the skipper said, 'Reckon he's no Jonah
after all, eh? Tew an' a 'alf cran we fetched aboard, young 'un,
an' thet's about th' 'andsomest cetch I ever remember off o' this
'ere beach.' And when it came to be talked about later on, as such
matters invariably were, none of the old-timers could bring to
mind a better haul. So in every way my first voyage was a
memorable one.

There were, of course, plenty of fish about in the early 1920s.
Four years of war had given them a welcome breathing space and
in the North Sea they had spawned and multiplied till there was
an abundance of every kind. Fishing had continued during hostilities though on a very limited scale so that over large areas they
were left to themselves. No great fleets of drifters and trawlers
came out hunting them night and day; the job of these tough
little craft had been to sweep up and destroy enemy mines.

I was a mere lad in breeches then down on the Norfolk coast
but I still remember how excited I got whenever the beach boats
were launched, piled high amidships with brown herring nets, and
how I used to trudge along the shore watching the line of corks
getting longer and longer as one man rowed slowly while his two
companions threw the nets into the sea. When they were all out
I'd see the crew settle down and light their pipes or maybe take a
swig from the bottle of cold tea they always seemed to have with
them. And so they would quietly drift, carried by the flooding
tide, up past Scratby and California towards Caister and Great
Yarmouth. By now it would be getting dusk and reluctantly I had
to wave them good-bye and head for home; mothers then didn't
allow their nippers to prowl about alone at all hours of the night.

But I would go to sleep wondering how they were getting on,
what luck they were having out there on the dark sea with only
the flashing beams of the *Cockle* lightship for company. Then,
long before anyone else was awake, I'd be dressed and down on
the beach hoping to see them come in; but usually I was too late.
I'd find every boat drawn up on the sand, stools either side to

keep them upright, mast, sail and oars stowed along the thwarts, nets stacked on barrows or flaked down to dry, but never a fisherman to be seen. It took a long time for me to understand that because herrings were caught in the dark, fishermen had to do their job while we were all asleep and had generally finished their day's work by breakfast-time.

Soon after the war had ended my father bought an army hut that had been used by the coastal defence forces and converted it into a pleasant summer house. It was at Hemsby and stood on top of the dunes, which flank the beach for miles on this part of the coast, and was about the first of what later were called 'seaside bungalows'. There were, I remember, one or two tarred, wooden sheds tucked away in hollows among the marrams, but these belonged to the fishermen and were used for stowing their gear.

The village of Hemsby was a mile inland and consisted of a handful of pebble-stone cottages, a pub, a church with a very high tower making a prominent day mark for shipping, and a small railway station where once or twice a day a yellowish-brown locomotive with glittering brasswork would stop to pick up the odd passenger for Great Yarmouth. The carriages were, I believe, also brown and, like the engine, very spick and span.

The older fishermen, whose neat little cottages had tiny front gardens displaying a profusion of multi-coloured begonias in summer, generally walked the mile to the beach though sometimes you would see them perched up in a farm tumbril if it happened to be going that way. These were men of 50, 60 or 70. The youngsters, those in their 20s, 30s or 40s, mostly just demobilised from the Patrol Service, preferred the less arduous and more speedy progress of the bicycle.

There must have been some ten or a dozen boats working regularly off the beach, some of them doubtless of a ripe old age, but all well cared for and painted in the distinctive fashion of the district. Their bottoms were tarred, sides painted white almost without exception, gunwales a vivid red, green or blue. My favourite had always been Y.H.62. If she had a name I have forgotten it, I always referred to her by her registration letters and number which showed she was a Yarmouth boat. Nor can I now remember the name of her owner–skipper though in my mind's eye I can still see his kindly, weather-beaten face, blue eyes and a mouth always ready to part in a smile. I couldn't understand at first why sometimes weeks would go by and I'd never see him, then I learned that he spent most of his time in the steam boats sailing out of Great Yarmouth. But whenever he was home from a trip he'd be down on the beach pottering around Y.H.62. and if the weather allowed he'd be off with a fleet of nets as if he couldn't abide kicking his heels ashore when there was the chance of earning a few shillings. It was one such time when he lifted me into the boat and took me on my first voyage.

There were others whose names, strangely enough, do come to mind though I never knew them as intimately as Y.H.62. There was Durrant who had two boats which I remember particularly because unlike the others their bottoms were red and their top-sides yellow. He didn't live up in the village but in his hut on the dunes, with a red-headed woman who seemed to be quite a few years younger than himself. They seemed to spend most of their time beachcombing and amassing great piles of driftwood, so that it was something of an event when he launched off to do some fishing. Then there were the Knights, the Cheyneys and the Halls, several to each family, who seemed to combine longshoring with work on the land, no uncommon thing in those days. One of the Halls I remember most clearly: he was short but strongly built with piercing grey eyes, invariably wore an old blue guernsey with more darns than stitches, and walked the district hawking bloaters which he'd salted and smoked in his back-yard. If anyone demur-red about the price (ten for sixpence I think it was) he would let fly a stream of unsavoury, and to a youngster, quite horrifying language, replace the oily bit of canvas over the fish in his basket, and stomp off in search of more amenable customers. He must have been well over 70 but had the agility of a cat and thought nothing of pushing a shrimp net, with water up to his chest, for two or three hours at a stretch.

My friend Y.H.62. was much younger, as near as I can tell in his early 40s, and quite a different type from the bloater seller. He nearly always wore a cap, with a shiny, cheese-cutter peak, after the style of those favoured by the old-time engine drivers, while over his guernsey, except in the hottest of weather, he had a smartly-cut reefer jacket of pilot cloth. He was quiet spoken and never used in my presence what was called then 'bad language'. Being a boy the thing I probably liked most about him was that he never minded me hanging round his boat doing odd jobs like putting the fish into peds, clearing the crabs and seaweed from the bilges or using my meagre strength to help with a launching. He never made me feel I was a pest or in the way, which on many occasions I'm sure I must have been.

Launchings, especially if the sea was a bit choppy, were the highlights of my young life. The boats, or more correctly punts, were about 17ft long, clinker built of oak, and were heavy things to get into the water when loaded up to the gunwales with nets, or perhaps lines, boles, dan-buoys, ropes, anchors and oars. In addition there was the stout pine mast, already stepped, and the thick canvas lugsail. A line of well greased wooden skids was laid down the beach for the iron-bound keel to slide on and with a man either side to hold her upright she'd be pushed over the gently sloping sand till she was just awash forward. Then any last minute items would be put aboard such as the bottle of tea and a few hunks of bread and cheese, when everyone caught hold to shove her afloat. I'd helped to do this many a time and nearly always got soaked going in up to my waist for a final push.

At quite a few places along the coast there were capstans for hauling the boats up again but Hemsby boasted no such luxuries so anyone willing to give a heave was more than welcome and usually had the reward of a fish or two. I soon learned that in a small fishing community there can be no question of every man for himself; all have to pull together. If they didn't there could be no fishing as working off an open beach is arduous and exacting, often demanding the combined efforts of everyone to avoid a calamity that could easily involve the loss of boat, gear or even life.

When the crew had given her a good offing with the oars we'd see the rudder being shipped, the sail hoisted and the whole boat heel gently to the wind. She was away to the fishing grounds and how envious I was! At such moments my one idea of heaven was to be on board, sailing far out into that wide expanse of sea I'd only gazed on from the shore. That's real adventure, I'd say to myself, different from the rot you read about in boys' books.

Well, as I've already described, I did make it in the end, thanks to my good friend Y.H.62., who subsequently proved as good as his word and often let me go with him when he was home from the big boating. But besides actually going off there were plenty of other things for an eager youngster to do, like fishing with hand lines. He had given me some lengths of stout twine together with a handful of dab hooks and shown me how to tie them to the snoods and attach the snoods to the line. He helped me make up three lines, about thirty or forty yards long, with ten or a dozen hooks on each, and then sent me searching the beach for medium sized stones with holes in to act as sinkers. Those of just the right weight took a bit of finding but I got them at last and we tied them to the end of the line. Next, I had to beg, borrow or steal an old broom handle into one end of which we drove a nail three-quarters of its length and cut off the head with a hacksaw. 'There ye are, sonny,' he said, 'all ye want now is a morsel of bait an' ye'll soon have a fry up for yer supper.'

A morsel of bait! The only kind I'd ever used was bread pressed round the point of a bent pin when trying to catch minnows; somehow I didn't think that was what he had in mind.

'Some nice lugworms, now, that's what yer really want,' he said, 'but o' course yer don't get 'em 'ere on this bit o' th' coast, much tew sandy, only find 'em round t' th' norrard, Blakeney, Cley an' them places where there's plenty o' mud.'

'Must we have worms?' I asked, timidly.

He took a puff at his clay pipe, or diddle, as they were more rightly called hereabouts, presumably because they would still be sucked long after they had burnt out, rather in the manner of a baby's dummy. Ashore they were generally smoked with the full length of stem, but at sea you'd find it broken down to a mere stump so that the bowl was close to the mouth and less likely to get caught in nets and gear.

'No, sonny,' he reflected, 'yew don't by any manner o' means hev t' hev worms. As good a bait as anything is a nice, thin strip o' herrin'. Dew yew look in th' boat now, under thet old garnsey o' mine, mebbe yew'll find one.'

And sure enough, under the guernsey there were three fine longshores he must have put aside specially when he came ashore that morning. I brought them to him and taking out the clasp knife he invariably carried in his right hand reefer pocket he touched it up on a large pebble stone lying handy and laying the herring on a bit of wood cut the whole length of the backbone, brought the knife back, and neatly removed a fillet. Then, turning it over, he did the same on the other side. Throwing away the bone, which soon attracted the attention of a large black-headed gull, he cut the fillets diagonally into strips about half an inch wide. The three fish produced thirty or forty strips, more than enough for the three lines. Taking one of the hooks in his right hand and a strip of herring in the other he pushed the point through the flesh and skin at one end and about an inch down brought it back in reverse order through skin and flesh.

'There y'are,' he said, holding it up for me to examine, 'th' fish'll start nibbling away at the bit hanging down there (he pointed to the piece suspended below the bend of the hook), then he'll take a big bite, seeing as 'ow he likes th' taste of it, when he'll be bound t' take the hook as well, an' yew've got 'im.' He smiled, as if relishing the look of doubt on my face. 'Thas right enough what I'm tellin' on yer, yew'll see. But dew yew dew t'others now.'

Rather gingerly I took up the next hook and at first was all fingers and thumbs; I couldn't get the point through the tough skin and lost most of the fleshy part in the sand. But slowly, and after pricking myself a good few times, I got the hang of it and eventually finished off the last line to an approving nod from my tutor.

I straightened my back grinning with satisfaction and feeling very proud of myself. 'Can we go fishing now?' I asked, bursting with excitement to catch something. 'Yew could,' he replied thoughtfully, 'an' then agen yew couldn't. Yer see, it's broad daylight, an' yew don't catch much then. Be better when it begins t' get dark. An' th' tide's ebbin' now, tew, no good fishin' on th' ebb,

B

never catch nowt then, better wait till th' flood begins to make. Anyhows, I'm off now t' brew meself a mug o' tea, dew yew be down agen in about a couple o' hours, we'll 'av a go then.'

Whereupon he stuffed some black shag into his diddle, lit it with an ingenious lighter contrived from a small shell case (a relic of the war as he afterwards told me), took up my lines one after the other and tied a loop about four feet from the stone. The first hook was some six feet from this loop.

'What's that for,' I enquired, a bit mystified.

'That's so as yew can cast it. Look. Here's th' broom handle with the nail. We put the nail threw th' loop, like so'—he took the handle, put the loop over the nail and held it out—'now, if yew stand facin' along the beach t'ards Scratby an' start swingin' gentle like, yew'll see how easy it be to hull it forty or fifty yards.'

But he didn't 'hull' it (a delightful Norfolk verb meaning to throw). He put everything down and made off for that mug of tea which he was going to make over a smoky old oil stove in his shed, or 'shod', to use the longshoremen's vernacular. As he drifted away I wound my lines on to three bits of stick and went in search of something to eat and drink myself, for out in the sea air all day I had 'the appetite of a hunter', as my mother used to describe it.

Even so those two hours passed like an age. My chief concern was to find a dilapidated rush basket, in common use then for shopping, which was hidden away somewhere in a cupboard. It would be just the thing to hold all those fish I was going to catch! It was big enough I feel sure to have taken 12–14lb but I never gave that a thought; for a more optimistic fisher than I never set foot on a beach when, at the end of that interminable two hours, I went to re-join my friend. I saw him walking towards Y.H.62. with those sliding kind of steps all longshoremen adopted in those days where the beach was sandy and soft; they never lifted the feet and plonked them down as visitors did, thereby sinking in up to the ankles. They walked as if they wore snow shoes and could tramp for miles without any signs of weariness.

That evening, for by now the sun was beginning to go down

over the marrams, I had my first lesson in the art of cast-line fishing. The method, as I soon learned, was to cast one line, move fifty yards and cast the next, then another fifty yards and cast the third. It took about ten minutes to get them all in the water when we strolled slowly back to the first and began hauling it in. This was the moment I'd been waiting for! For although my friend had done all the casting he handed me the line to pull in. I was so excited I just dropped it anywhere; on my own I should soon have had everything in a complete tangle. But my mentor took over for a moment and showed me how to flake it down in neat loops up and down the beach all ready for casting again.

'Mustn't ever have a foul line, sonny,' he explained, 'always pay it down so's when yew let that there stone fly it'll carry the line out clear without any snags.'

Anxiously I took the line again and thought it wasn't coming in quite as smoothly as it had been. I must have hesitated. 'What's the matter?' he asked. I gave a pull. 'Don't know, it seems to be wobbling about, you feel.'

He took the line in one hand, changed the position of his dibble with the other, and grinned at me. 'Go yew on, lad, heave away,' he said, giving it back to me, 'reckon as how yew've got sumthin' first go.' Sure enough, through the waves came a flurry of splashes as I hauled in my first longshore fish, which turned out to be a sizeable red gurnard. Most likely I did a war dance round my trophy, I can't remember now; but I'm sure it was that moment which kindled the interest I have retained over the years in sea fishing and above all, in the skill and endurance of those men who follow this fickle calling and, summer and winter alike, bring their catches to our tables.

That night the two of us, man and boy, plied the lines till long after dark and it was only the thought of my mother wondering what dire trouble I had got into that made us give over at last. But any fear I may have had of a scolding disappeared as I lugged home the rush basket which had in it, besides the gurnard, two or three dabs, an eel, one horse mackerel and three plaice. Here was a meal for the whole family—and I had caught it!

After that never-to-be-forgotten initiation I lost no opportunity of working my lines and in a week or two got fairly proficient at casting, though being a nipper I could never equal the mighty throws achieved by Y.H.62. I carried on when he was away in his big boat out of Yarmouth and seldom came back empty handed. Nor did I neglect to keep an eye on the punt and see the stools were fitting snugly under the bilges in a heavy blow. Strong winds quickly loosened them making the boat rock which was all unnecessary strain. Between trips he'd sometimes be home for a day and a night and never missed a stroll on the beach to see his boat. Nor did he fail in his customary greeting of 'Well, sonny, how are yer and how's the fishin'?' It made me feel as if already I was a hardened longshoreman!

Besides the fishing there was always something interesting happening on the North Sea in those days. Mines were still a menace and the sweepers had to be constantly at work clearing them up. Those that came to the surface were spotted by men sent aloft in kite balloons from the decks of small warships. Many a time I watched them patrolling in the roads between Caister and Winterton Ness. The *Cockle* lightship, anchored some $3\frac{1}{2}$ miles from the shore and right opposite us, was my boon companion and I would gaze at her for hours, in fair weather and foul, tossing and heaving at her moorings. Many small coasters then hoisted sails if they had a fair wind and there was great excitement when one of them would be seen from the *Cockle* to be taking a dangerous course likely to put her on a sand bank; then the lightship would fire a warning gun and run up a hoist of flags. If you chanced to be looking you would see a puff of whitish–grey smoke but it would be quite a while before you heard the sound of the explosion. This long remained a mystery to me till my father explained it was all to do with the difference in the speed that light waves travelled (seeing the puff of smoke) and sound waves (hearing the bang).

On very clear days there was another lightship I could look at, the *Newarp*. She was twelve miles away in a north-easterly direction and marked what we called 'the outer roads'. I was able to study her, and everything else that appeared, through a fine telescope my father kept on two brackets above the doorway. It had,

I believe, done duty on the poop of a clipper ship and was powerful enough to bring passing vessels right into close-up. When the
sun was round of an afternoon it glinted on the *Newarp's* sides
and I could just make out the big white letters forming her name.
But usually it was only her three masts I could see topped by their
basket-like day marks. I thought it a pretty lonely place for a ship
to be anchored in and wondered what sort of life her crew led
tossing about all that way from the shore.

'It's not that bad,' said one of the younger fishermen to me
once, who had himself served in the lightships for a time, 'you're
never short of fish for a start, there's always a line or two hanging
over the side and out there in deep water there's plenty to be
caught. Then there's reading, you've plenty of time for that when
you're off watch, though most of the chaps prefer to have a go at
a bit of model making. Some rare pretty little things they turn
out, too, mostly of the lightship herself, but if any passing ship
has taken their fancy they'll maybe try their hand at that.' Years
later, in some of those delightful glory holes you found in the old
Yarmouth Rows, I picked up quite a few of these lightship
models, many broken with all their rigging gone, and spent end-
less enjoyable hours repairing them and painting in the most
turbulent putty seas.

The full-rigged ship was not a common sight in the 1920s but
with the telescope glued to my eye I followed the course of more
than one though they were always a long way off and their hulls
were barely visible. Warships were another matter, there seemed
to be no end of them dashing up and down the coast, usually in
the *Cockle* channel, so I had a good view of them. They looked
splendid in their grey paint creaming the water at twenty or thirty
knots and if I was the first to sight one, perhaps coming up round
Winterton Ness or down past Caister, I'd rush in shouting,
'Daddy, a battleship! Look! Over there! A great huge one!' My
father was closely connected with naval construction and would
generally smile tolerantly as he followed my gaze to the ship in
question and tell me she was not really a battleship but a torpedo-
boat-destroyer, or maybe a light cruiser. Of course, I had never
seen a battleship then and knew nothing about the difference

between one class and another, but their passing, whatever they were, always caused a flutter of excitement. In those days our admiration for the navy knew no bounds.

When Joseph Conrad, in later life, described the North Sea as 'the schoolroom of my trade', he meant, I think, that it was from the east coast sailors and fishermen that he took his first steps in the mastery of the English language, which afterwards he was to make his own. He had only the scantiest knowledge of our tongue when he came ashore at Lowestoft from the ss *Mavis* on 18 June 1878, though we may assume it improved during the four weeks he was kicking his heels in the port looking for a berth. There he would have come in daily contact with the smacksmen, driftermen, bargemen and wherrymen, though he must have found the East Anglian dialect pretty hard to understand. When he eventually shipped aboard the *Skimmer of the Sea*, a collier owned by Joseph Saul of Lowestoft, his shipmates were all Suffolk men, excepting one, hailing from places like Pakefield, Corton and Lowestoft, and with names still common in the district like Cook (master), Chandler (mate), Boon (able seaman), Munnings (able seaman), Goldspink (able seaman) and Barham (boy). After serving for ten weeks and making three round trips between Lowestoft and Newcastle his English had improved sufficiently for him to answer an advertisement offering berths in a wool clipper bound for Australia. This letter of application was his first attempt at written English; it was successful for it led to his joining the *Duke of Sutherland* as an ordinary seaman, the beginning of his deep-sea career. Nearly forty years later he came back to Lowestoft, to do some propaganda writing to help the war effort, and went to sea for a few hours in one of the smacks being fitted out as a 'Q' ship. He must have looked with considerable nostalgia at the harbour filled now mainly with steam-driven ships of war instead of his beloved schooners and brigs.

I used to enjoy Sunday evenings down on the beach when fishing was slack, the sun warm, and an air of peace pervaded everything. For then, after church or chapel, some of the real old-timers, men of 80 or more, whose whole working lives had been spent afloat, would shuffle over the dunes, seat themselves gratefully on an unused net barrow, fill up their clays, and begin to mardle.

'Saw ol' Josh t'other day,' one might begin, to be questioned by another of the venerable company with, 'Be yew ameanin' thet there Josh what used t' be aboard th' *Newarp* light all them years?' Most probably that would be the one referred to when the first speaker, after a moment's pause and an all-embracing look to seaward, would continue by recounting some incident in the life of that fellow shellback who had first seen the light of day little more than twenty years after the battle of Waterloo. I was all ears for such tales especially those to do with my much-loved lightships. One I recall was about the *Newarp*, though whether Josh was aboard her at the time I cannot say.

''Twere a darkish night,' said the very old longshoreman, in a voice I can only describe as frail, 'but not what yew'd call thick. Given good eyes yew could see a couple o' mile, but they couldn't 'a bin lookin' aboard thet there steamboat. I've heard say she were out o' Lundun bound down Whitby way, but how some maybe, she went slap bang int' th' *Newarp*, which being th' ebb was heading sutherly, stove in her bow plates, smashed all along 'er side an' brought down the light. Took them chaps an hour t' rig a new 'un. A rum do thet were an' no mistake. Merciful thing they weren't all drowned. O' course, soon as th' Trinity come out they knew as how she'd have to be docked, so it weren't long afore she were replaced. Could never fathom how it come to happen. Might be some sort o' excuse for a sailin' craft, but this 'ere were a steamboat.'

'Did they ever get to knowin' the name o' th' steamer?' someone enquired.

The old one thought for a moment trying to cast his mind back half a century. 'Yes,' he said at last, 'I think as how they did. Funny soundin' name if I remember right, something like Caredmon, yes, that were it, Caredmon, though arter all this 'ere time I couldn't rightly swear t' it.'

In fact his memory was not very wide of the mark for the incident in question occurred on the night of 10 April 1878, and the vessel which collided with the *Newarp* was the ss *Cædmon*, of Whitby. But how inappropriate that a ship bearing the name of a Saxon poet should have been guilty of such negligent navigation.

There was another collision story I liked, this time involving the *Cockle*, because it all ended happily, though for the chief participant it must have been a very embarrassing experience. Towards the end of November 1897 a fierce north-westerly gale swept the Norfolk coast and one of the many vessels forced to run for it was the ketch *Lord Wolseley*, of Shields, bound for London. What manner of trouble she got into no one could say, except that off Hemsby she somehow ran foul of the *Cockle* lightship, both vessels being locked together for several minutes. Her master must have thought that this was the end as he hauled himself over the side of the lightship just in time to see his ketch break free and go scudding off before the gale. Soon she had disappeared into the murk and both her master and the lightship's crew had little doubt she would founder with all on board. Later, the Caister lifeboat was launched and brought the master to Great Yarmouth, where he was suitably cared for. Three days elapsed then, literally out of the blue, a telegram arrived saying the *Lord Wolseley* had safely reached the Downs and been towed into Ramsgate where she was now lying, awaiting the return of her master! After the long, if comparatively comfortable, journey from Great Yarmouth to Ramsgate by train, I feel that the skipper must have had quite a red face as he stepped on board.

Wrecks and strandings have for centuries been the natural order of things on the Norfolk coast in bad weather and news of a calamity was more often than not regarded as a godsend. In the hard times of last century the casting ashore of a vessel usually meant some welcome salvage; tallow, maybe, to make candles; a bolt of worsted that would provide clothes for a family; rope to rig a boat with; while a tub of gin or a cask of French wine, not to mention a 10lb pack of tobacco, could bring a hint of luxury to lives accustomed from birth to all that was rough and raw. While things were hard enough in the 1920s there was not the desperate poverty of a hundred years before; most children had boots, breeches and shirts and their tummies were well provided for by mothers who were at home all day and not out to work. They had

time to bake home-made bread from flour ground in the local
wind- or water-mill, could contrive wholesome broths from marrow bones and vegetables out of the garden, and had not lost the
art of making Norfolk dumplings which, as I remember them,
were as big as small footballs and as light as a feather. With broth
and a few chunks of beef they made a main dish; sprinkled with
sugar a delicious 'after'.

Even so, when I was a youngster you found few staying indoors
if there was talk of a wreck within ten miles of our bit of the
coast; there was bound to be something useful washed up. I
know I'd be down on the beach from morning to night kicking
through the raffle along the tideline on the look out for anything
worth carrying off. For some reason I greatly prized nice new
planks and baulks of timber, though why I don't know as I was
much too young to make anything with them. Possibly it was the
look of them, all butter-yellow amongst the dark sand and seaweed. Many's the one I've lugged great distances and delivered
in triumph to my father, and sooner or later when there was a job
to be done about the place they would be put to good use. For if
you lived along the coast you never thought of buying timber.
Outside every dwelling you'd see great stacks of driftwood, most
destined for the grate, but the best lengths put aside to make a
new chicken run, a bigger hutch for the rabbits or a more substantial privy down the end of the garden. I seldom came back
from a beachcombing ramble without my pockets being stuffed
with half-used lengths of candle; before electricity reached the
coast oil lamps and candles provided all our light but this was one
commodity my mother never had to buy. Candles were still being
used for ships' lights and presumably when the lamp trimmer got
to work in the morning he threw overboard any unburnt pieces
that he reckoned wouldn't see the next night through. I, and a
good many others, reaped a rich harvest from all those discarded
bits.

But from an early age I had been told that if I found anything
really valuable I must report it to the coastguard. Small things
didn't count but big items that were obviously worth a lot of
money came under the protection of someone called the receiver

of wrecks. Unfortunately, nothing of this nature ever came my way although I constantly had visions of augmenting my weekly sixpence with some salvage money.

One occasion I recall was when a vessel got into trouble and soon after the beach was strewn with wooden tubs of new potatoes. My mates and I had great fun dashing into the water and rolling them up the beach. Those that weren't broken were put together in piles and eventually carried away in carts, presumably to be looked after by the receiver of wrecks. However, a great many tubs had split open and for several days potatoes came bobbing ashore by the thousand to be gathered up in sacks, bags, baskets and buckets by the village folk. Oranges, too, once drove ashore in huge quantities but they weren't so popular as they had been in the water some time and the salt had got into them.

One blowing day in autumn I noticed some unusual activity on the beach and immediately went to investigate. Everyone, I discovered, had their eyes on a boat, just beyond the breakers, with nobody in, which I gathered was off some ship; quite a worthwhile piece of salvage. It was an unwritten law on our coast that the one who first laid hands on an object was the rightful claimant to any reward that might be paid, so there was keen competition among the fishermen to get a touch of her. She came in fast driven by an easterly wind and was at last caught up on the top of a big breaker and came sweeping in right on to the beach. A dozen strong arms seized her gunwale, some skids were brought along, and soon she was resting safely well above high-water mark. I never discovered who it was got the salvage money for her, indeed I don't think any was paid, for some time after one of the fishermen brought down a few pots of paint and in a couple of days she was resplendent in the green, white and black of the other beach boats. It seemed that either the owners could not be traced or were not interested in regaining possession of her, and accepted a modest pound or two to be rid of her. Whatever it was, there she stayed for as long as I can remember and no doubt in the fullness of time crumbled to pieces or was broken up like all the others. But before that happened she was often at sea and landed many a good haul of herrings.

Youngsters, it is said, have little sense of fear, and during stormy weather I certainly never realised in what danger it placed the ships I could see wallowing bows under through my telescope. I found it exhilarating in a hard north-easter watching small coasters, drifters or trawlers plunging through the seas, showers of spray flying high over bridge and funnel. These struggles were to me grand and exciting spectacles and I gloried in the sight of their stems crashing into wave after wave as cascades of water surged over their f'c'sles and their decks became a smother of foam. And I remember wishing I could be on board to experience these battles myself, to feel the pitching and rolling and to have the taste of salt spray in my mouth. For never did it cross my mind that these ships might not survive the ordeal or come safely to port. Most of them did; but some, like the *Hopelyn*, did not.

On 19 October 1922, a hard blow came on from the north-east and during the night a steamer ran aground on the Scroby Sands. These sands flank Great Yarmouth and Caister and the deep water in between forms the famous Yarmouth Roads. From Hemsby the Scrobies are clearly visible at low water away to the south-east, but on this occasion no sand could be seen only a boiling mass of broken seas. As night came on the wind seemed to increase and for us safely behind doors it was good to light the lamps and tuck into a hot beef pudding.

But there was no such comfort for the men of the *Hopelyn* though at the time we knew nothing of the drama that was being played out only a few miles away. Not till breakfast did we see the stranded ship and then the murk made it impossible to discover what was happening. However, I did know a bit about lifeboats, how they were manned by the longshoremen and would go off in the most terrible weather when a ship was wrecked and I felt sure the one at Caister would already be out giving all the help she could. I had often walked along the beach and seen her lying in her shed on the dunes, shiny white and blue, ready to launch off the moment she was needed. Though only a boy her sense of power and her look of grace and beauty had always impressed me and I was glad to think that now she was out in her natural element rescuing the sailors from that stranded ship.

But, sad to say, as I learned later, she was never launched as the weather was too bad to get off the beach and it was the Gorleston boat that went. She courageously stood by the wreck all night and part of the next morning, only returning to harbour when no one was seen on board and it was presumed all had drowned. Soon after she got back, however, the Caister coastguard reported a flag flying from the *Hopelyn* so, exhausted as they were after ten hours at sea, the Gorleston men returned to the wreck. Only the bridge and two stumps of masts showed above water but they anchored close by, being unable to get alongside by the buckled, jagged plates and the remains of another wreck nearby. Then the lifeboat herself hit the sands, was damaged and had to return to harbour once more.

Meanwhile, a third attempt at rescue was being made, this time by the Lowestoft boat, and they met the Gorleston men coming away. After laying to for a few moments the Gorleston coxswain volunteered to join the Lowestoft boat but by the time she reached the *Hopelyn* it was dark and they could do nothing but anchor and wait for daylight. The men cooped up on the bridge of the wreck, where they had gathered as a last refuge, with great seas continually breaking over them, must nearly have given up hope as the second long night fell upon them. But seeing the lifeboat anchor they may have guessed she would stand by till the dawn came bringing a ray of cheer through the dark hours. There were twenty-four of them all told, the entire ship's company, besides the cat, for those men had heart enough to see she had an equal chance with themselves.

And when daylight did come they were saved. The lifeboat veered down on her anchor and lay alongside for the crew to slide down ropes into her—one manfully clutching pussy to his breast. Then hauling up to her anchor again and cutting the cable the lifeboat got clear of the sands and was soon safely in harbour. It was an epic rescue, one still spoken of on the east coast, and the men who so gallantly stood to their task through two nights and three days, were the longshoremen.. In the eyes of one small boy at least they were heroes.

The loss of the *Hopelyn* remains firmly fixed in my memory

because for a long time afterwards her rusting bridge and a section of mast remained sticking gauntly up out of the sea. It was a sinister reminder for passing ships that the Scroby Sands must be given a wide berth in fair weather or foul. I was glad when at last the wind and the waves took their toll and these gruesome remains disappeared from the scene.

Needless to say many other ships besides the *Hopelyn* met with misfortune, one I remember, the *Castle Galleon*, ended up right on our doorstep so to speak, but no lives were lost and she was eventually re-floated. Thames barges, too, often got into trouble, but generally speaking as new ships with more powerful engines appeared wrecks and strandings became less frequent.

There were, as I have already said, few full-rigged sailing ships to be seen in the 1920s but there was no dearth of sail using the ports of Great Yarmouth and Lowestoft. London and Rochester barges were regular visitors; Scandinavian timber arrived in a variety of medium-sized Baltic coasters, still hoisting a goodly spread of canvas for all their auxiliary engines; wherries carried all kinds of cargoes up the rivers Yare, Bure and Waveney; while there were yet the smacks working out of Lowestoft, some of the finest sailing craft to be found anywhere round our coasts. There was a host of smaller fry relying on sail and oar, practically all the beach boats as well as the shrimpers from Yarmouth and South-wold, and the first tiller I ever had in my hand was Y.H.62.'s when her great lugsail was up. So most youngsters were sail conscious in a quite remarkable degree and liked to consider them-selves real little authorities on the handling of boats under canvas; I suppose I was no exception. As I grew older and stronger, able to pull an oar, hoist sail and steer, I was always able to get a berth when the herrings showed up in autumn. October and November were hectic months, especially at Great Yarmouth and Lowestoft, when the harbours were jammed tight with tier upon tier of local and Scotch drifters. My father got little peace at this time because I was constantly badgering him to take me down to the fish quays so that I could watch the boats leaving and coming in, see the catches being landed and the industrious Scots lassies gutting, smell the sea tang of the nets and listen to the rorty language in all kinds of dialects. These sights, sounds and smells were a joy to my young heart; just to be there was very heaven.

In casting my mind back over the years I have tried to give a glimpse of longshoring life as I knew it; of the men; of the boats they went to sea in; of what they did and what they talked about; perhaps, too, of how small boys grew up. I cannot say if I was typical of my generation but I do know that since that time my interest in fishing has never waned.

The catching of fish is an occupation that reaches far back into the past; a calling, as I believe, that is, truly, as old as the hills. How it began I shall attempt to show in the next chapter.

# CHAPTER TWO

# The First Fishermen

Few of us these days eat fresh-water fish; the thought of fried rudd and chips, tench pie or marinated barbel hardly gives an edge to our appetites. Trout, admittedly, still appear in the fishmongers' shops but most of these are imported from Scandinavia. Yet in the dim and distant past the first fish to be caught and eaten were taken from inland waters, from rivers, lakes and broads, which covered a much larger area and were probably deeper than they are now. Also, the word pollution had not then been heard of.

The seaboard had few attractions for communities engaged mainly in agricultural pursuits and the sea itself was generally thought to be worthless, barren and entirely unproductive. That, certainly, was Homer's idea. So we can, I think, imagine our early ancestors going down to the river side when in search of fish, though how exactly they caught them remains a matter for conjecture. Most probably a barrier was put across the smaller streams, constructed of brushwood roughly woven between stakes, that would let the water through but trap the fish. These could be retrieved by the simple expedient of diving in after them. Nearer the coast, where rivers were tidal with a consequent rise and fall in the level of the water, they could be collected when the tide went down. As coastal areas came more into favour as places of habitation when it was realised that the sea did, in fact, contain vast quantities of fish, the barrier idea was no doubt modified by erecting it on the beach in the shape of a V, the point facing in the direction of the ebb, so that fish swimming into this trap would become stranded as the tide left them. Such 'engines'

persisted well into this century so the principle behind them was
obviously a good one.

The stop net, used in the Thames estuary as late as the 1890s. It dates back to
the time of primitive man when he built barriers of stones and branches across
streams and small rivers

The idea of a net most likely came from watching how fish got
entangled in the woven brushwood of the barriers. Pointers to its
antiquity are provided by remains which have been discovered in
prehistoric Swiss lake villages, and in examples using the same
knot as in Europe, to be found all over the world among civilised
and primitive people.

These means could have provided enough fish to feed a family
and, perhaps, a community, but a more individual method was to
use a spear, a natural progression from its employment as a hunting weapon. It would have been eminently suitable for taking
large fish like salmon in the clear, upper reaches of rivers, and it
certainly served for this purpose, in some areas of Britain, till the
turn of the present century.

The hook, with bait attached, probably came later when the
feeding habits of fish were better understood. There seems to

(*above*) Cromer, Norfolk, about 1910, with some of the double-ended boats typical of this stretch of coast

Page 33

(*below*) Long liners at Cromer before World War I. The holes in the top strakes served in place of rowlocks and after coming ashore the oars were run through these holes enabling the boat to be carried bodily up the beach

*(left)* Scudding a heavy catch of sprats at Kessingland, Suffolk, between the wars. They were usually shaken out on to a tarpaulin or old sail kept for the purpose

*(right)* Estuary craft arriving at Billingsgate in the early hours of the morning with their catches, 1883

have been no problem in contriving these out of thorns, bones or even shells, for among the artifacts of coast-dwelling tribes, in both hemispheres, fish-hooks abound, some fashioned with remarkable skill.

Two references in the Old Testament show that 2,700 years ago methods we know today were in common use, the hook (angle), the drift-net (net) and the trawl or seine (drag). The confusion of Egypt as prophesied in Chapter 19 of Isaiah tells what the fate of the longshoremen shall be: '8. The fishers also shall mourn, and all they that cast angle into the brooks shall lament, and they that spread nets upon the waters shall languish. 9. Moreover they that work in fine flax, and they that weave networks, shall be confounded. 10. And they shall be broken in the purpose thereof, all that make sluices and ponds for fish.' We may construe 'sluices' in this context as barriers, already discussed, while 'ponds' were man-made pools for keeping fish alive until required.

Chapter 1 of Habakkuk has to do with the vengeance of the Chaldeans who regarded other peoples as of no more account than fish. By ignoring the simile of the following two verses, which is intended to show the ruthlessness of the Chaldeans, we gain a further insight of how fishing was conducted. '15. They take up all of them with the angle, they catch them in their net, and gather them in their drag: therefore they rejoice and are glad. 16. Therefore they sacrifice unto their net, and burn incense unto their drag; because by them their portion is fat, and their meat plenteous.'

Nowadays, nets produce nearly all the fish we eat, the spear, or harpoon, being mainly confined to whale catching, while the hook finds favour almost exclusively among beach anglers. The immense catching capacity of the net has made it indispensable for meeting the present day demand for fish. The increasing scarcity of fish is another factor. Where they are plentiful the hook is adequate but where they are few and far between great areas have, literally, to be swept clean to produce anything in the way of a catch. What the days of plenty were like I shall hope to show in due course though I fear we shall never know them again.

C

Yet a few years ago I was given a glimpse of what seas full of fish are like when cruising off the south island of New Zealand.

My companion asked his wife how the tucker was and she replied that half-a-dozen blue cod would do all right for supper. So we got under way down the sound and reaching deep water cut the engine. I expected the anchor to go down but was assured there was no need of it as ten minutes would suffice to catch all we wanted. Each of us had a line with three hooks which we baited with a lump of decaying squid knocking about in the bottom of the boat. Over went my line and I waited for the lead to thump on the rocks beneath us. As it did so I felt a tug and straightaway hauled in. To my astonishment there was a cod on each hook but before I could get them all over the side a barracuda shot up and carried off half of the lower one. 'That's the trouble here,' said my companion, 'those 'cudas think you're fishing just for their special benefit. Anyhow, throw those two back, they're too small.'

Both would have turned the scale at 2lb or more but I did as I was told, let go my line again, and turned to see my friend bring in a beauty about 5lb. In less than the ten minutes we had our six fish though we must have thrown back a couple of dozen 'undersized' ones. For good measure, and eventual use as bait, we had three or four big barracudas as well. No one eats these as they are reckoned to be full of worms.

My face must have betrayed the disbelief I felt at having got our tucker so easily and swiftly. 'How does that compare with the Old Country?' my companion enquired with a grin as we headed back up the sound. Of course there was no comparison and I told him so. Yet 200 years ago, or even less, fish were just as plentiful round our British coasts.

Catches were taken along the beaches and close inshore because there was no need to go further, and strange as it may seem now, the object was not to catch as much fish as possible but only sufficient to meet the needs of the community, often a sparsely populated hamlet of a dozen or so cottages. As there was little communication with other places, and that along rough or muddy tracks, there was no opportunity of finding a market inland. So, in much the same way as the miller made flour from the grain grown round about, so did the fisherman catch only what his neighbours wanted or could afford. Longshoring followed the pattern of most other cottage industries in those distant days when life went on in closely-knit communities and every village had its own identity.

This and a great deal more was swept away as roads were improved and with the coming of the railway a network of communications was developed up and down the country able to bring fish speedily to the large inland cities where previously it had been a rarity. Once roads had been made fit to walk on the fishwife could take her husband's catch and peddle it round the adjoining countryside; so now he went out to catch more fish than was actually needed by the local community. Better roads also meant that waggons could trundle short distances carrying baskets of fish to neighbouring places and arriving in time for it to be edible; fish is a perishable commodity and had to be eaten as soon as possible after being caught, especially in summer.

James Murie, in his *Report on the Sea Fisheries of the Thames Estuary*, published in 1903, speaks of how the Leigh-on-Sea fishermen got their catches to Billingsgate about the year 1820. 'A Mr. James Cook,' he records, 'commenced to run vans nightly from Leigh to London. These vans were large, open vehicles, wherein were placed the shrimp "pads", viz, oblong, lidded baskets, and bags of oysters or other fish as the case might be. Each pad would hold from eight to ten gallons of shrimps and they were packed one above the other, a tarpaulin covering the lot, and the driver perched on a high seat in front. The vans started from the "Billet" Wharf between 6 and 7 p.m., occasionally later, even to 9 o'clock. With considerable excitement they were driven four-horsed up the steep hill of the village, then two or three horses took on the load according to its weight or the condition of the roads. They went by Wickford and Shenfield. At the latter they changed horses and arrived at Billingsgate between four and five the next morning.'

Before vans like this started running supplies reached London by sea. Boats sailed right up to the quay at Billingsgate and in the early hours of the morning—the market opened for business at

5am—presented a noisy and lively scene with craft jockeying for position, fish being humped ashore, oaths flying as a vessel jumped the queue, auctioneers ranting and costermongers haggling, bent on driving a neat bargain. The salty tang inseparable from sea fish pervaded all, mingled with the reek of coffee stall and ale house.

Billingsgate was ideally placed flanking the Thames for the great river was not the stinking thing it is today. Its water was wholesome and fish of all sorts thrived in it; salmon, sturgeon,

Thames smacks at work in the 1870s

smelts, lampreys and a host more. Longshoremen worked regularly round the Isle of Dogs and in other reaches netting sprats and whitebait, while below Gravesend whole fleets of small boats went out after plaice, soles, skate, cod, flounders, oysters and shrimps. Of all the longshore and inshore fisheries those in the

Thames estuary were the best placed because they had a ready market close at hand and with so many mouths to feed in the metropolis could profitably dispose of everything caught. (See page 34.)

On more distant stations, however, the story was different, the limited demand, as we have seen, keeping catches down to quantities that could be sold locally. I have mentioned how plentiful fish used to be round our coasts and here is an instance given in 1848 by W. Brabazon in his *Deep Sea and Coast Fisheries of Ireland*. 'On the West Coast,' he says, 'the very great poverty of the fishermen arises from the want of markets or other demand for fish. The fishermen often see the creeks along the West Coast crammed with fine fish, when they could take tons of them at a haul, with a deep seine or drift net, but when caught they would be useless to them as they could neither salt nor sell them. I have been told by an inspecting officer of the Coast Guard that he has several times seen herrings on the coast of Donegal sold for ten pence per thousand, which would make two barrels of herrings, worth in the Dublin market two pounds ten shillings.'

At Crail, on the Fifeshire coast, a shoal of herring once swam in so closely packed that by dipping a basket or bucket half-a-dozen fish could be drawn out. The fisherfolk flocked to the harvest and despatched the public crier with the glad news that fine fresh herring could be had at forty a penny. As the tide rose the fish swarmed in even closer and baskets could be filled at a dip. So the crier had to announce that a cartload could be taken on the foreshore for one shilling. Few availed themselves of this offer and at last the people were invited to take all they wanted for nothing. Eventually the glut became so extraordinary that it was impossible to deal with it. At high water a huge mass of herrings had accumulated and as the tide left them vast numbers remained on shore unable to escape. As they began to rot the local authority in desperation was forced to offer a shilling to anyone carrying away a cartful and so most were removed by farmers and used for manure. Had there been any means of getting them to market the people of Crail would have reaped a rich harvest as all the fish were full and in prime condition.

Sprats frequently appeared in enormous shoals and once, towards the end of 1854, they gathered in a solid mass outside and inside Galway docks and on several nights rose to the surface in such numbers that the people took them up in hampers which they filled with one scoop. A contemporary account relates that 'they died eventually in such quantities that the stench was abominable for weeks'.

I could quote many other instances showing the abundance of fish that once surrounded these islands but the above may be enough to show how it was possible for men fishing off the beach to earn a passable living without needing to go long distances out to sea. This, as we shall see later, only became necessary as demand increased and the inshore grounds became exhausted.

Fishing as a distinct occupation probably developed from the simple collecting of shellfish along the shore after which would have come the improvising of some crude vessel to go afloat in and the fashioning of implements to catch different fish. The net, the spear and the hook could easily have been adapted for use from a log, dugout or boat. There would have been those who favoured this kind of activity just as others might have preferred tilling the soil, rearing livestock or hunting. In this way small, compact communities would have grown up, each member making his own contribution to the common store.

It is, I think, significant that up to little more than a hundred years ago very similar communities existed on the coasts and my belief is, that apart from growing bigger, they had remained largely unchanged for centuries. Even today you find coast villages where the clan instincts die hard; where any new resident is regarded as a foreigner for twenty years or more; where marriages are frowned upon should bride or 'groom come from another parish; and where inter-breeding has persisted so long that deterioration of mental faculties is evident.

The early coastal communities seem to have been of varying stock. In Leone Levi's *Economic Condition of Fishermen*, published in 1883, we read: 'Go a little deeper into their nationalities and you find them everywhere a peculiar people. Scandinavian blood is evident among the north-eastern fishermen,

Phœnician blood among the Cornish, Spanish blood is seen among the Galway fisherfolk, and especially in the Claddagh.' Again, F. E. Sawyer, in *Sussex Fish and Fisheries*, 1882, says: 'The Sussex fishermen are a mixed race, partly Spanish, partly Norman French, partly Teutonic in origin.'

James Murie, from whom I have already quoted, lived in Leigh-on-Sea at the turn of the century and made a thorough study of the Thames estuary fishermen. He knew them intimately for many years and this is how he speaks of them: 'There is considerable interest attached to the fishermen inasmuch as their physical and mental trait is doubtless affected by their race. Origin and surroundings furnish an index to their character generally. . . Speaking in a broad sense, the majority of the Leigh fisherfolk are of fully average size, muscular, well-built men and good examples of their craft. There are a few extra tall and some short and thick set examples, but quite a minority in number. Prevailing colour of hair is dark brown or chestnut, the eyes blue of [different] shades. There are others showing the Saxon trait of fair hair and light blue eyes, even one family of cocklers partial albinos. There is also a sprinkling of freckled, ruddy-skinned Dano–Germano type. Again there are some in which dark hair and hazel brown eyes [may indicate] Norman blood . . . Some of the family names such as Cotgrove, Emery, Johnson, Kirby and Jossermin point to the patronymics of the above races. Possibly the Anglo–Saxon element predominates.'

There are grounds for thinking that in some cases groups of people shipwrecked on the coast, miles from any habitation, had no option but to make the best of their situation, like Robinson Crusoe, squatted where they were, began scratching the soil to produce crops, built small boats from the wreckage of their ships and in time became accepted as natives. We may find it hard to believe that this could have happened when practically every mile of coast has its quota of caravans and beach huts, but these are of recent origin, no older in fact that the motor car. Coastal areas two or three centuries ago were bleak, sparsely populated and uninviting.

The now almost legendary 'fisherman's cottage', reasonably

well built and often poised, rather precariously one would think, only a biscuit-throw from the sea's edge, dates from little further back than the beginning of last century. Before then the coast fishers lived out a comfortless existence in rude abodes no better than hovels. We can turn to Murie again, writing in the 1890s, for a glimpse of what some of them were like. He records: 'Originally the fishers' dwellings on the beach [at Leigh] must have been little better than shanties; for men now living remember some of the old wooden houses ... sunk in the ground, so that two or three steps had to be descended to their entrance, and they had no upper storeys.'

At about this time, 1801, the first census was taken in Leigh when the population was shown to be 570. Two-thirds were considered to be fishermen and their families or others relying on the sea for a living. By 1891 the census showed the population had nearly quadrupled, being returned at 2,108, but only one-third were now engaged at sea. Although the proportion of fishermen to the population had decreased, their numbers had almost doubled in ninety years. It was no doubt this increase in population, creating a bigger local demand, and improving facilities for getting catches to Billingsgate, that produced a better return for the fishermen so enabling them to build better houses. If this be true of Leigh it is probably true also, to a greater or lesser extent, of other districts.

It is difficult to assess with any accuracy what fishermen earned 100 or 150 years ago but an indication that it was no more than a pittance is provided by Robert Fraser who, in 1818, published *A Review of the Domestic Fisheries of Great Britain and Ireland*. Therein he relates that at Arklow, in the county of Wicklow, there were then 45 boats, each with 6 hands, employed in the herring fishery. Around 80–100 mease of herrings were caught by each boat in a season and were sold at an average price of 14 shillings a mease. This measure, sometimes written mace, is a quantity of 500. If we take 90 as the mean, each boat would have grossed £63 for the season, and assuming the 6 hands were on equal shares, they would have received just over £10 a head, or a little more than 4 shillings a week if spread over the whole year.

Besides wear and tear on nets and boats they had to pay £3 a year for their 'cabins' on the beach, which may have been dwellings like the ones at Leigh, but were more likely sheds for stowing gear. Some paid a shilling a year ground rent and built their own cabins from wreckage picked up on the beach. When the herrings were finished, work was found for the children making and mending nets, most of them never seeing the inside of a schoolroom, while their fathers went dredging for oysters which were carried across to Liverpool and sold. With what they got for them they bought coal, earthenware and such-like essentials. It was a hard, hand-to-mouth existence and but for unlimited supplies of fish they must have starved.

English and Scottish fishermen never knew the poverty that was all too common in Ireland and by the third quarter of last century had achieved a reasonable standard of life. Leone Levi, in the work already quoted, estimated that by about 1880 a fisherman had roughly 9 shillings a week to support his family which then numbered four or five persons. I have included a table he prepared relating to such things as marriage, illegitimacy, pauperism, etc at the chief fishing centres, from which he makes the following observations: 'As a whole, as respects house accommodation, the fisherfolk are somewhat better off than the entire population, though more crowded at Hastings, Margate and Ramsgate. They marry at an earlier age than the entire population and this is more especially seen at Yarmouth and Grimsby, whilst there is reason to believe they intermarry among themselves to a large extent. The rate of illegitimacy is somewhat less among the fisherfolk than among the entire population but an excess is notable in Yarmouth and St. Ives. As may be imagined, the rate of mortality is less in the fishing ports than in the whole of England, except at Yarmouth. Pauperism is likewise less among the fisher-people than among the entire population but the rate is high at St. Ives, Yarmouth and Lowestoft. There is less drunkenness, too, among the fishing population, as indicated by the rate of committals to prison for the same except, indeed, at Grimsby. But, as might be expected, the amount held at the Savings Banks in the fishing ports is less than among the entire population partly, doubtless, because they do not save much but, especially, because a large proportion of the savings of fishermen is invested in the building of fishing boats.'

| Fishing Ports | Number of persons to inhabited house | Proportion per cent Married under age per 1000 | Proportion of Illegitimate per cent | Rate of Mortality | Rate of Pauperism | Rate per 1000 of Committals for Drunkenness | Amount at the Savings Bank per head |
|---|---|---|---|---|---|---|---|
| Whitby . . . . . | 4·84 | 14 | 3·77 | 18·3 | 32 | – | 26/ |
| Grimsby . . . . | 5·09 | 18 | 4·70 | 17·2 | 23 | 9·50 | 13/ |
| Hastings . . . . | 6·63 | 10 | 4·36 | 17·9 | 25 | 1·58 | 33/ |
| Margate* . . . . | 5·65 | 17 | 4·41 | 18·2 | 22 | 5·03 | 54/ |
| Ramsgate* . . . . | 5·38 | 17 | 4·41 | 18·2 | 22 | 7·91 | 33/ |
| Yarmouth . . . . | 4·56 | 22 | 6·82 | 22·6 | 33 | 4·52 | 108/ |
| Lowestoft† . . . | 4·88 | 17 | 3·27 | 16·2 | 33 | 4·06 | 53/ |
| St Ives . . . . . | 4·34 | 14 | 6·53 | 17·7 | 40 | – | 12/6 |
| Average of fishing ports | 5·17 | 16 | 4·78 | 18·3 | 29 | 4·90 | 44/ |
| England and Wales . | 5·37 | 14 | 4·80 | 20·5 | 31 | 6·70 | 52/ |

* Registration District, Thanet          † Registration District, Mutford

I have already mentioned their dwellings which, if not lavishly furnished, at least kept out the weather. James Purves, at times a rather flowery chronicler, contributed the chapter on 'The Northern Shores' to Clark Russell's *The British Seas*, published in 1894. I quote the following description as it allows us to look back nearly a hundred years and see how longshoremen lived on the Firth of Forth.

'The interior of a fisherman's house,' he says, 'is worth seeing. You find crockery, wall ornaments and bits of pictures that are nowhere else to be seen; they reflect the simple taste and peculiar idiosyncrasies of the fisher folk. The huge, well-filled bed, with heavy curtains, though stuffy looks decidedly inviting and made to remain in, as it is difficult to get out of; you often surprise a fisherman resting there during the day, and as he rises on his elbow reproduces the picture of the poor wayfarer and his wife that of the good Samaritan. In front of the bed, as a seat, is the husband's chest, holding his Sunday clothes. Above the dresser or kitchen table and on the plate-rack are ranged in rows dinner plates of various makes and colours, and hung round the beams on nails are milk jugs, all in pairs; I have counted in one house as many as a dozen different patterns. These plates and jugs are not for ordinary daily use but for the picturesque ornamentation of their walls. On the mantelpiece and on shelves are many stoneware figures, brilliantly coloured, generally Portobello ware, representing shepherds and shepherdesses in Arcadian guise, sailors and their sweethearts in everlasting embrace, Burns and Highland Mary, the Babes in the Wood, Napoleon and the Prince Consort, with underneath appropriate snatches of poetry, and Delft dogs in the very picture of health and gorgeous hues, look contentedly down. There are pictures, such as Raising the Widow of Nain's Son, a shipwreck and the rescuing lifeboat, and a cheap print of the Queen—and in a window corner the family are photographed, the men in working garb, the women carrying creels on their backs, all justly proud of their calling. In the corner stands the antique, well-filled corner cupboard containing their best tea set, used on high days and family gatherings. Stout antique brass candlesticks set off the ends of the mantelpiece. Each house has its framed memoriam cards of those who have been drowned.

'Sometimes they possess an inner apartment—"the room"— with another huge bed and a substantial chest of drawers with spiral pillars. A large family Bible is placed on the table covered with a crimson cloth; and on the hearthstone is a homemade, many-coloured rug. In the garret and about the kitchen are stowed away nets and fishing gear. Round fish creels and long, shallow creels with coils of lines resting on beds of freshly cut grass, each line with a hundred or so of hooks baited with bits of bright-coloured sand-worm or glistening clam, lie about the house or the door ready for the goodman (as the husband is called) going to the sea.'

The illustration of womenfolk with creels on their backs (a creel was a large basket for carrying fish) mentioned by Purves, shows how closely concerned the whole family was in the business not only of catching fish but of selling them. The wives and

Newhaven fishwives, 1860

daughters, helped by the children, went out every day digging lugworms and gathering mussels and clams for bait; they baited their menfolk's lines as soon as they got in from sea, ready for the morrow; they braided and mended nets; knitted long stockings and thick jerseys; but above all they took the fish and went off to sell it round the countryside.

The most famous of these 'fishwives' were undoubtedly those from Newhaven, near Edinburgh, who obviously took the fancy of George IV as he declared them to be the handsomest women he had ever seen; Queen Victoria said she 'viewed them with eyes of wonder and admiration'. J. G. Bertram, in his *Harvest of the Sea*, 1865, wrote of them thus: 'Before the railway era the Newhaven fishwife was a great fact and could be met with in Edinburgh in her picturesque costume of short but voluminous and gaudy petticoats, shouting "Caller herrings!" or "Wha'll buy my caller cod?" with all the energy that a strong pair of lungs could supply. Then, in the evening, there entered the city the oyster-wench, with her prolonged musical aria of "Wha'll o' caller ou?" But the spread of fishmongers' shops and the increase of oyster-taverns is doing away with this picturesque branch of the business. Thirty years ago nearly the whole of the fishermen of the Firth of Forth, in view of the Edinburgh market, made for Newhaven with their cargoes of white fish; and these were all bought up by the women who carried them on their backs to Edinburgh in creels and then hawked them through the city. The sight of a bevy of fishwives in the streets, although comparatively rare now, may still occasionally be enjoyed; but the railways have lightened their labours and we do not find them climbing the Whale Brae with a hundredweight, or two hundredweight, perhaps, of fish to be sold in driblets, for a few pence, all through Edinburgh.' For those not acquainted with the Scots I might mention that the cry 'caller' means simply 'fresh'.

The hard, slogging work done by these fishwives was proverbial but they accepted it without demur. Their philosophy could be summed up in the words of one of them, 'the woman that canna work for a man is no worth ane', while there is the story with much the same bearing of one rather delicate Newhaven lass who was about to get married. On hearing of it another girl, a strapping specimen of eighteen, said feelingly: 'Jenny Flucker taking a man! She's got a gude cheek; who is she tae keep him? The puir man'll hae tae sell his fish as weel as catch them!'

Fisherrow, a little to the east of Newhaven, had another fishing community which did business in Edinburgh. The women from there had a considerably longer walk than those from Newhaven but were not held in quite the same esteem. The Newhaven wives always regarded themselves as the queens of their profession and Dr Carlyle of Inveresk, writing in the 1860s, testifies to their hard work. 'When the boats come in late to the harbour in the afternoon,' he says, 'so as to leave them no more than time to reach Edinburgh before dinner, it is not unusual for them to perform the journey of five miles by relays, three of them being employed in carrying one basket and shifting it from one to the other every hundred yards, by which means they have been known to arrive at the fish market in less than three-quarters of an hour. It is a well-known fact that three of these women went from Dunbar to Edinburgh, a distance of twenty-seven miles, with each of them a load of herrings on her back of 200 pounds, in five hours.'

The word 'fishwife' used to have a rather unfortunate connotation suggesting hard bargaining and language of no great delicacy. Yet the majority were God-fearing and church-going, though by the nature of their trade they seem to have been inhibited in their devotions. The story is told of a clergyman who numbered many of them among his parishioners but was concerned at how the majority never partook of the sacrament. Eventually he enquired the reason for this neglect and was told with great frankness that because their trade led them quite often to cheat and tell lies they felt themselves unfitted to join in that particular religious duty.

The practice of women selling the fish caught by their menfolk was not confined to Scotland, though in other places they went under different names. In Dublin there was the famous Molly Malone peddling her cockles and mussels, though with a wheelbarrow she no doubt found it easier than humping heavy baskets. We need not enquire whether she really existed or was just a poet's fancy; certain it is there were plenty of her kind a hundred years ago making the streets of the 'fair city' echo with their cries. But Molly was a 'cadger', not a fishwife. This was a name used all over Ireland for men and women who bought small lots of fish and sold them for the best price they could get. 'Jolter' was also commonly used and had much the same meaning.

Cornwall's peregrinating fish sellers claimed the unusual name of 'jowder', their special line being pilchards and mackerel which they lugged inland for miles from places like St Ives and Mevagissey (see page 52). Sussex had an even more unlikely word for its fishwives, 'jugg', which may possibly derive from the Dutch 'juk', meaning a yoke for carrying buckets or baskets. Many set off from Hastings and Brighton and though often loaded with mackerel and herring they did not neglect the flatfish and cod when any were to be had cheaply.

The 'costermongers' of London were a somewhat different breed being simply itinerant retailers. Many of them were women and they plied their trade with plenty of cockney wit generously sprinkled with 'Billingsgate'. Every day they filled their baskets or barrows with fish from the market, two or three often joining together to buy in bulk so saving a penny or two. Then, dividing it up, they would be off 'crying' it round all the poorer districts. Most of the prime fish found its way to the West End but if you wanted freshly-boiled shrimps, cockles, winkles, whelks and such-like humble delicacies, then it was to the East End and the coster-mongers you went. Originally, costermongers were those who sold the large costard apple, often as big as a baby's head and of delicious flavour, but the name was eventually applied to all street sellers in London.

'Hawkers' and 'hucksters' were found more in country districts and here again we find both words coming from the Dutch, 'heuker' being someone who offers goods for sale in the street. The need for fish to be sold as fresh as possible was long recognised in law and from as far back as 1698 it was allowed to be cried in the London streets on a Sunday. As recently as the Pedlars Act of 1871 and the Hawkers Act of 1888, fish sellers were made exempt from obtaining a licence.

What to do with fish after it is caught has always been a problem; it is so perishable that in the height of summer it will go off after forty-eight hours and be unfit for human food. The task of preserving fish has, over the centuries, demanded almost as much ingenuity as catching it. Refrigeration has now solved the matter so successfully that practically everything offered for sale ought to be fit to eat. In the early days as we have seen the abundance of fish was no boon to the fishermen as they could not dispose of it fresh and had little means of preserving it. The simplest efforts in this direction must have been to dry it in the wind, after chopping off the head and removing the guts, as experience would have shown that these were the first parts to decay.

Wind-dried fish persisted till quite recent times. In Cornwall they used to stick a branch into the ground, smooth the twigs, then spit mackerel on them to dry with the help of wind and sun. In Exeter High Street a fishmonger called Gosden sold whiting obtained from the Dartmouth fishermen which had been dried in the sun; they were called 'buckhorn' and found great favour as a breakfast dish. Forty years ago in all the coastal villages of Holland it was quite common to see dabs and small plaice, headless and finless, stuck on thin sticks and put outside houses, usually by the front door, to dry. I remember once having a dish of them grilled for supper in the island of Ameland after a blustery crossing from the mainland and they were excellent.

The value of salt as a preservative must have been recognised very early on. For hundreds of years it remained the most common and reliable of all methods and made possible the curing, as it was called, of practically every kind of fish. Long before Cheshire salt was known many coastal places built salt pans, flat areas over which the tide was allowed to flow then, the sea being excluded, they were left to evaporate leaving behind a considerable deposit of brownish-coloured salt. This would either be rubbed into the flesh, a process known as dry-salting, or a solution would be made and the fish put in to soak, called brining. In the first method they were eventually laid to dry in the open air when they became as hard as boards, the 'stock-fish' which older readers will remember being on sale during the last war, along with snoek and whale-meat sausages. Cod salted and dried in this way is an accepted dish in Portuguese restaurants but bad cooking, so typical of the country, ensures its appearance as a most unpalatable mess.

Brining, or pickling, was especially useful for preserving herring and mackerel and I will deal more fully with this in the next chapter. The discovery that smoke had a preservative action as well as improving the flavour of the fish probably came much later, perhaps even by accident. The once famous Finnan haddock originated in the chance hanging up of two or three to dry over a peat fire; when taken down they were found to be so tasty that they were afterwards prepared regularly in this way. The bloater, too, was an accidental discovery as I shall show later.

The use of ice, to cool and thereby preserve, fish may be attributed to the demands of the Scotch salmon fishery. Up to about 1800 the sale of this much esteemed fish was limited to the

(*above*) Estuary fishing boats bearing away in a squall    *Page 51*

(*below*) A Great Yarmouth curing house. Herrings being roused in salt, washed, spitted and carried to the smoking room

*(left)* A Cornish jowder, 1900

*(right)* '. . . a man standing on the extreme edge of a precipice just over the sea. . .' A Cornish huer

districts where it was caught. Much higher prices could be realised on the London market so much of it was cured or smoked; large quantities were boiled, steeped in vinegar and packed in small tubs. But after lengthy journeys to Billingsgate by boat or waggon what it made was only a fraction of the price obtained for fresh salmon. It was about 1780 that a Mr Dempster, of Dunnichen in Scotland, showed that ice suitably applied could keep salmon fresh and without loss of flavour for quite a long time. After this the salmon trade made rapid strides and with the coming into service of steamboats and railways every part of the country could be assured of fresh salmon whenever it was in season.

Finally, the best method of all to ensure fresh fish was to keep them alive in sea water till they were required. Several ways of doing this became popular, the first, undoubtedly, being the fish-pond, or 'stew'. They were often found on country estates, stocked with carp, while most religious establishments had them due to fish being mandatory on Fridays demanding regular supplies. Later, the pond was brought into commercial use to hold flat-fish, particularly flounders, cod, turbot, lobsters and various other kinds. At Leigh-on-Sea they were called 'store-pits' and measured about 120ft by 30ft. They were banked round with puddled clay and had 5 or 6ft of water in them which the tide kept fresh by an arrangement of inlet and outlet pipes. Turbot were put into these pits with a string tied round their tails and a cork on the free end which enabled the fishermen to know just where they were when required. A drag net was used for hauling out other varieties but some flounders would burrow so deeply into the mud that they escaped capture for a long time. James Murie records that when eventually taken many of them had attained a great size. Old-time winters were proverbially more severe than they are now and during long spells of frost the shores of the upper Thames were frequently ice-bound or so frozen over that the London fishers could not work their seines. 'Such times,' says Murie, 'were the Leighmen's opportunity. The store-pits were drained, the ice broken, and every fish on the muddy bottom was dragged out of its retreat... They were smartly conveyed to market and the fishermen rejoiced at the high prices obtained.'

D

Because fish, with the exception of eels, die fairly soon after being caught, boats were built with 'wells' through which the sea water was allowed to circulate. In simple terms, two watertight bulkheads were constructed roughly amidships, the sides of the vessel being here perforated with holes of an inch diameter. The fish were put into this well as they were caught and would stay alive without any marked deterioration for several weeks. When the water round our shores was unpolluted a boat could lie at anchor or alongside a quay, scooping out fish when needed because purchasers knew they would be perfectly wholesome and would give good prices. To save boats lying idle catches were more often than not transferred from the wells to the store-pits, though small batches would generally be put in 'chests', coffin shaped receptacles drilled with holes, in which the fish remained surviving as well as they did in the boats.

Such, then, were the main activities of fishermen ashore, after the fish were caught. Work enough to be sure, but we must turn now to the other half of the story and see how the catching was done, beginning with the fish that was once the staple of our British industry, the herring.

# CHAPTER THREE

# Shoal Fish—1. Herrings

In this and the next chapter we shall consider the three main kinds of what I call shoal fish: herrings, mackerel and pilchards. As the term suggests, they congregated in enormous numbers round our shores and because they swam in compact masses could be easily caught. Their whereabouts was not difficult to discover; pilchard shoals could actually be seen from the cliff-tops, appearing as a reddish-brown blur on the surface, while herrings and mackerel nearly always attracted flocks of sea birds in search of food. Another indication was the oily look they gave to the water accompanied by a smell which keen nostrils were quick to detect. The old-time fisherman was a dab hand at weighing up all these signs and deciding just where to shoot his nets. This ability has largely passed away now that boats have electronic means for pin-pointing fish though you still meet skippers with a healthy contempt for such 'new-fangled contraptions'.

For centuries the herring was called 'the king of the sea', not on account of its size but because it appeared in such plenty. Fishermen on the east coast of Scotland relied on it almost entirely for their livelihood, it was sought all along the north-east coasts of England, off the shores of Norfolk, Suffolk and Essex, in the English Channel and in Irish waters.

The universal method of catching was by drift-net, so called because when in the water it was free to drift with the tide. A good beach boat would carry anything from ten to twenty nets, each 30 or 40yd long, which were joined together to form a 'fleet'. They could be three, four or even five fathoms deep, and were supported by corks placed 3ft apart along the backrope. Some-

times, but not always, a footrope ran along the bottom with small
lead weights clamped on which helped to keep the net vertical.
Nets without footropes were preferred in shallow water because
if they came foul of any obstruction on the bottom a few meshes
would be torn away but the net itself would be saved. For herring
the meshes generally ran at 32 or 34 to the yard, a fraction over
1in square.

A Great Yarmouth lugger lying to her herring nets

Herring fishing was done at night because then the nets were
invisible but I have known the time when you could shoot half-a-
dozen nets in broad daylight and still take fifty or a hundred fish.
To mark the shoreward end of the fleet a buoy with a pole
through it carrying a hurricane lantern was used. At intervals
other buoys, or 'buffs', usually made of canvas and blown up with
air, marked the trend of the fleet, while the boat herself was
secured to the seaward end and was allowed to drift with the nets.
Four or five miles might be covered in this way and all the time
herrings swimming along the coast would strike the curtain of
netting and become 'gilled'. The mesh was large enough to let
the head through but not the body, any backward movement
resulting in the gill covers becoming caught on the side strands

of the mesh. Small and immature fish could, however, pass right through without injury, a great point in favour of the drift-net; it never took young, undersized fish and so stocks were conserved. Herrings today are dragged from the sea with giant trawls which make no distinction between mature and immature fish. The scrawny specimens offered for sale these days bear witness to the way they are caught.

It was a common custom on the east coast as the first net was thrown into the sea for the skipper to call out, 'In the name of the Lord'; and as the first one to be hauled in was touched he would say, 'Now for the Grand Secret'. Often the 'Grand Secret' was a very scanty show of fish but I never heard these expressions without feeling admiration for the simple faith of men who genuinely believed it took something besides their own skill to reap the harvest of the sea.

Important as the herring fishery was to the east coast, to Great Yarmouth and Lowestoft in particular, most landings came from deep-water boats; but being concerned mainly with the doings of longshoremen I must pass over the activities of the big luggers and, more recently, the steam and motor drifters, to see what part the beachmen played. In fact, they caught a somewhat different kind of fish, the once famous 'October herring' which swam close in to the shore, was quite small, full of fat and perfect for making the well known 'Yarmouth bloater'. Great care was taken in choosing prime fish for bloatering, hence the good price long-shore herring always made. Many fishmongers in places a short way inland bought them on the market early in the morning, salting and smoking them on their own premises, so that you could eat bloaters for tea which had been swimming off Hemsby or Winterton only twenty-four hours before.

When the fish were really swimming it was possible for the beach boats to make substantial hauls. One night I went off from the Suffolk coast with eleven nets which I began shooting as soon as we were afloat. My mate rowed out gently as I threw over the remainder, then we lit our pipes and pulled back to the 'pole end', the buoy with swaying lantern marking the first net. The buoy was afloat all right but the corks of three nets had disappeared,

sunk with the weight of fish in them. We had 'pinned' a dense
shoal swimming close up to the beach and as we started to haul
in, as carefully as possible, we could feel the nets tearing under
the strain. We eased them in as best we could but by the time we
had got the last one our freeboard was down to a few inches. We
had serious doubts about being able to beach without filling her
up but fortunately it was flat calm and we got her in safely. Even
so, with the weight of nets, the water which had drained out of
them and all the fish, it was a wonder she did not split open from
stem to stern as she lay on the sand. It was then about two in the
morning but it took us till after five to 'scud' the nets (shake out
the fish), box them up, spread the nets to dry and square up the
boat. By then we were ready for half-a-dozen grilled herrings
apiece, washed down with hot, strong, sweet tea.

Later in the day I watched our catch being auctioned at
Lowestoft, all told about a cran and a half, some 1,500 herrings,
not bad for a 14ft sailing boat. That same morning the deep-sea
drifters were returning from Smiths Knoll with about two or
three crans each, so we had been lucky. Being October longshores
our catch was bought for bloatering and as there were so few fish
on the market they made good money. Passing a greengrocer's on
my way home I bought several pomegranates, for we have a
saying on the east coast that they and the herrings are best when
they come in together.

Let us turn now to the villages on the eastern seaboard of
Scotland; here the longshoremen were all-important, catching the
greater part of the fish that kept the herring industry going. It was
a highly organised business and few went fishing for anything else
except herrings. It had the advantage of being a summer fishery,
lasting from early in July till about the middle of September, and
was based on the curing of herring for export. Less than a third
of the total catch was sold fresh, all the rest were salted, packed in
barrels and sent to the continent. Consignments also found their
way to the West Indies where planters fed them to their slaves.
With abolition this lucrative trade came to an end. In Europe,
Russia, Germany, Holland and Belgium were the principal purchasers and so highly prized were the early season Scotch pickled

herrings that in some inland German towns they sold for as much as a shilling each.

The need to salt them as soon as possible after they were caught led to the growth of a shore industry run by the curers in close association with the foreign buyers. This was complementary to, and indeed made possible, the activities of the fishermen. The curers contracted to buy all the herrings caught during the season while the fishermen undertook to supply the curers, with whom they had made agreements, with the fish they managed to catch. Usually a ceiling of 200 crans was placed on what could be taken and what delivered, the price being settled before the season started. Curers often advanced money on the contract to help the fishermen fit out their boats and see them through the hard winter months, but if the curers were small men with little capital, they in turn had to borrow from the buyers. All these arrangements were made at the end of one season ready for the next so the whole thing was largely a gamble as there was no telling when the time came if any fish would be caught. But such have always been the hazards and uncertainties of fishing although a hundred years ago the herring shoals were fairly predictable and it was seldom the Scotch catchers were unable to honour their bargains.

The obligations on each side were separate and clearly defined. The fisherman provided the boat, sails, nets, buoys, ropes and everything else necessary to obtain the fish, while the curer arranged for sheds and work-space, salt, barrels, coopers, women to gut and pack, horses and carts to bring the catch from the boat and reserved some open ground for drying nets.

When a curer began setting up a 'stand' or 'station' it was the signal for a motley collection of people to gather round; dealers in salt, sellers of barrel staves, vendors of cutch, overseas buyers, gutting lassies from inland and 'green hands' wanting to forsake farm work for a while and go to sea. Itinerant preachers and revivalists turned up to have their say and were mostly heard with respectful attention by the devout folk assembled. Many a prosperous little town was born in this manner, brought into being by the unseen wealth swimming with heaven-sent regularity along the coast every summer.

As June passed and the opening of the season drew on excitement ran high with everyone discussing the prospects for 'the fishing'. Boats which had been generously tarred and painted with the first show of mild weather were being put into final order; youngsters with rags were rubbing oil into masts and spars; the men attended the sails, stitching in, with palm and needle, a strengthening piece here or renewing a bolt rope there; the women, mothers, wives and sweethearts, were refurbishing old nets and braiding new ones. When finished, into the cauldrons of boiling cutch they went to steep and be made as rot-proof as possible; the sails followed and when taken out and dried they came out that soft, brown tint painted so lovingly by artists and eulogised so frequently by poets. A writer of those days remarked: 'The summer time of Wick's existence begins with the fishery; the shops are painted on their outsides and replenished within; the milliner and the tailor exhibit their newest fashions; the hardware merchant flourishes his most attractive frying-pans; the grocer amplifies his stock.' (See page 85.) From Buckhaven to Buckie it was the same; if the fishing was good all would prosper, or at least get through the winter, and for many a lass the success or failure of her laddie's boat would decide whether autumn would see her a married woman.

The fishing was done with drift nets as on the English coasts though many of the boats were larger especially if there was any sort of harbour for them to use. The biggest went to as much as 35ft on the keel and required a crew of five to work them with their mile-long fleet of nets. The majority were smaller and needed a crew of three only, often two men and a boy. Not all the hands were fishermen in the true sense as we learn from J. G. Bertram. 'By far the larger proportion of those engaged in the capture of the herring—particularly at the chief stations—are what are called "hired hands", a mixture of the farmer, the mechanic and the sailor; and this fact may account in some degree for a portion of the accidents which are sure to occur in stormy seasons. Many of these men are mere labourers at the herring fishery and have little skill at handling a boat; they are many of them farmers in Lewis or small crofters in the Isle of Skye.'

There are few such men left today though not long ago I met a *vigneron* on the banks of the Gironde who seemed to combine very successfully his work in the Médoc vineyards with a fair amount of estuary fishing. But one is reminded of those times by quite a few pubs called 'The Plough and Sail' whose signs often depict the close identity between work on the land and work at sea.

Although few Scotch herrings were disposed of fresh, where there was rail communication buyers did attend seeking supplies for Birmingham, Manchester and other inland cities. Consignments usually went off in open trucks with a tarpaulin as sole protection from sun, dust and flies, but in places far from the sea fresh fish, even if not as fresh as it might be, was a luxury and always in keen demand.

With the first landings of fish to be salted for export coopers and gutters got busy for speed was essential if the herring were to be barrelled in the best possible condition. To quote Bertram again: 'This process during a good season employs a very large number of persons . . . As soon as the boats reach the harbour— and as the fishing is carried on at night they arrive very early in the morning—the various crews commence to carry their fish to the reception troughs of the curers by whom they have been engaged. A person in the interest of the curer checks the number of crans brought in and sprinkles the fish from time to time with considerable quantities of salt. As soon as a score or two of baskets have been emptied the gutters set earnestly to do their portion of the work, which is dirty and disagreeable in the extreme. They usually work in companies of about five—one or two gutting, one or two carrying and another packing. Baskets full of the fish, as soon as they are gutted, are carried to the back of the yard and plunged into a large tub, there to be roused and mixed up with salt. Then the adroit and active packer seizes a handful and arranges them with the greatest precision in a barrel, a handful of salt being thrown over each layer as it is put in, so that, in the space of a few minutes, the large barrel is crammed full with many hundred fish, all gutted, roused and packed in a period of not more than ten minutes. As the fish settle down in the barrel more are added from day to day till it is thoroughly full. On the proper performance of these parts of the business the quality of the cured fish very much depends.' (See page 85.)

Skimped or slip-shod work was never tolerated as the following directions to the coopers show: 'During the period of the curing the cooper's first employment in the morning should be to examine every barrel packed on the previous day in order to discover if any of them have lost the pickle, so that he may have all such barrels immediately re-packed, salted and pickled. He should see that the gutters are furnished every morning with sharp knives. He should be careful to strew salt among the herrings as they are turned into the gutting troughs; give a general but strict attention to the gutters in order to ensure that they do their work properly; see that the herrings are properly sorted and that all broken and injured fish are removed; and take care that the fish are sufficiently and effectually roused. Then he should see that every barrel is seasoned with water, and the hoops properly driven, before they are given to the packers. He should likewise keep his eyes over the packers to see that the tiers of herrings are regularly laid and salted and that a cover is placed on every barrel immediately after it has been completely packed.'

The Scotch fisher-lassies did not confine their activities to Scotland but travelled southward as the herring shoals moved along the coast. They arrived in Great Yarmouth and Lowestoft towards the end of October and for a schoolboy, as I was when I first came to know them, it was quite an experience to hear the Scots tongue for the first time and the good-natured banter that was for ever going on between these often buxom, and equally often, handsome wenches, and all the assembled locals, fishermen, salesmen, carters, buyers, coal merchants, chandlers and a good many more.

I wish I could set down a conversation I once overheard between a Yarmouth drifter boy and one of the Scots girls he had a mind to take to 'the pictures'. It must have gone on for five minutes and at the end of it I'll wager neither had understood more than half-a-dozen words of what the other had said. In despair the boy returned to his boat, where he obviously had his leg pulled, while the girl was surrounded by her companions agog to know what the talking had been about. I hope they did eventually resolve their problem and saw Charlie Chaplin that night.

Wireless was then in its infancy and people's speech reflected the districts they hailed from and not the synthetic accents picked up from a loudspeaker. Language was earthy and robust, a delight to listen to in places like Great Yarmouth at the height of the herring season, when you could hear a bevy of dialects from as far afield as Cornwall and the Shetlands.

In due time wireless sets were carried by fishing boats chiefly for listening-in to the weather forecasts. A story I heard long ago told of two boats, each with a wireless, fishing about half-a-mile from each other. It was time for the morning forecast so the first skipper turns his rheostat (they weren't called switches then), dons his earphones and manipulates the coils. Slowly twiddling his condenser knob he at last hears a suave voice telling him what weather he can expect during the next twelve hours. When it's finished he hangs up the earphones, turns the set off and bears away for the other boat. Reaching a comfortable hailing distance he sings out, 'Ahoy, there, Jimma bor! Jest heard abowt th' weather on me wireless. My man giv' easterly winds, freshening. What did yours giv'?'

When preparing herrings for the frying-pan or grill the head is removed, the belly split open and the guts, with roe, removed. But those to be pickled and barrelled were treated rather differently, the head was left on and only the guts and gills removed. This was done by laying the fish in the hollow of the left hand with its head projecting about an inch beyond the fingers. The gutting, or 'gypping', knife (a short, sharp-pointed blade firmly set in a wooden handle) was held in the right hand and its point inserted into the throat, cutting down to the backbone and through to the other side when, by a dexterous movement of the fingers and turn of the wrist, the entrails and gills were removed. The operation demanded a really sharp knife otherwise a rough, jagged cut was made, unacceptable to continental customers.

Now and again I hear my obliging fishmonger enquire of a newly-wed housewife if he should 'dress' the two herrings she has just bought for tea; and I can't help smiling to myself when she replies with some such words as, 'Oh yes, do, please, I can't stand fiddling about with the messy things'. I wish she could have seen the Scots girls in their heyday, about eleven in the forenoon, troughs full from the night's catch, plying their knives with a deftness and speed impossible to describe. There was a bob down from the waist to seize a herring, the imperceptible thrust, twist and withdrawal of the knife, then a bob up to throw it into the basket; it took less time than it does to write, thirty or forty fish being accounted for in a minute.

It was in truth a hard and dirty job, carried on in all weathers with little or no protection from wind, rain and cold. But the girls were generally well prepared, girding themselves with thick woollen jumpers and scarves, topped by massive oilskin aprons enveloping the chest and reaching down to the ankles. Within ten minutes of starting work they were spattered from head to foot in scales, blood and guts, yet like as not as you walked by they'd be crooning a Scots air or chattering happily as if hard work were the sure recipe for contentment. Come the evening, however, when soap and water had done their job, and you would not have recognised them. With hair brushed, combed and done up in a bun at the back, decked out in a neat, if homemade, dress, the transformation was startling. In Great Yarmouth they lodged in houses down the Rows, those quaint, narrow openings leading from the quay which gave so much charm to the old town, and there they would sit in the doorways knitting as if their fingers had not had enough employment for one day.

In the Shetlands they made their temporary homes in huts built for the purpose, all sparsely furnished, and with sleeping arranged on the bunk principle as in a ship. Two, often three, girls would share a single bunk. Catering, cooking and cleaning were done on a communal basis. Being of self-reliant stock they made their own amusements, when they had time for any, and seldom omitted their devotions on a Sunday. Sad it is that one will never see their kind again; like most of the herring they have disappeared. The few fish still landed are gutted by machines which are passably efficient, quick and economical. But they don't sing as they work and no drifter boy would ever want to take one to the pictures.

With the title 'king of the sea' it is only natural that the herring should be surrounded with much lore and legend. Bygone fishermen called them 'North Sea pheasants' and when fried for breakfast in the big boats were eaten as often as not with a pungent liquid dubbed 'North Sea sauce'. So far as I remember it was made in a jug containing equal parts of sea water and vinegar to which a large tin of mustard was added and stirred in thoroughly. It was then bottled and used as required, being poured over the hot, steaming fish as they arrived from the galley.

J. W. de Caux, who published *Herring and the Herring Fishery* in 1881, recorded a number of the old fishermen's beliefs. 'Occasionally,' he says, 'herrings are caught, the fins of which are tinged with a beautiful bright red colour, whilst their bodies are suffused with a shadowy golden haze. By the Scotch fishermen these herrings are known as "wine-drinkers", by the fishermen along the coasts of Norfolk and Lincolnshire they are called "loaders", whilst by the West Country fishermen they are honoured by the appellation "kings and queens". Fishermen look upon these herrings as omens of success; as soon as one is perceived it is taken from the net, carefully prevented from touching anything that is made of wood, and at once passed round the scudding-pole as many times as the fishermen desire to get lasts of herrings at their next haul. Unsalted herrings, some twenty-four hours after their capture, present a dark red appearance about the gills and fins; but this cannot be the cause of the appearance of the wine-drinkers, loaders or kings and queens as fishermen assure me that they are sometimes captured alive in which case, after having been passed round the scudding-pole, they are at once returned to their native element. Unsalted herrings of this description are called in the trade "overday-tarts", but sharp costermongers recommend them to their customers as being "bleeding new".'

As might be expected the herring appears in song and in one ditty takes his place alongside several other kinds in proffering advice to an apparently unwary fishing skipper; but I am not sure whether this advice was intended for the skipper's good or to prevent him catching the fish. The omission of the 's' from the present tense, third person singular, in 'how the sea roar', suggests that it is of East Anglian origin. It was sung to a simple, rousing tune and sounded well in the four-ale bar through a blue haze of shag tobacco smoke. There are innumerable verses, almost as many as there are fish in the sea, but four will suffice, I think, to show what the fish had in mind.

> Up jumped the Mackerel with the fork in his tail,
> He said to the Skipper, 'You'll soon have a gale',
> > Singing, stormy old weather boys,
> > How the sea roar.
> Chorus:    Stormy old weather boys,
> > How the sea roar.

> Up jumped the Sprat with his pretty back,
> He said to the Skipper, 'You're on the wrong tack',
> > Singing, stormy old weather boys,
> > How the sea roar.
> Chorus:    Stormy, etc.

> Up jumped the Cod with his ugly fat head,
> He said to the Skipper, 'Take a cast of your lead',
> > Singing, stormy old weather boys,
> > How the sea roar.
> Chorus:    Stormy, etc.

> Up jumped the Herring the King of the Sea,
> He said to the Skipper, 'Put your helm hard a-lee',
> > Singing, stormy old weather boys,
> > How the sea roar.
> Chorus:    Stormy, etc.

It was pleasant in the Great Yarmouth of fifty years ago, especially during late summer and autumn, to see all the little fish shops with neat wooden boxes of freshly-smoked bloaters which you were invited to send as gifts to friends. You knew they had come straight from the quayside to the smoke-house at the back of the premises and had not been twenty-four hours out of the water. For a modest sum of about one-and-sixpence, which included postage, you could despatch a dozen fish confident that they would arrive at their destination in time for breakfast next day.

The fronts of fishmongers' shops were mostly open then and on the marble slab would be assembled inviting heaps of 'wet' or fresh fish, just out of the boats. But above, on toffee-coloured spits or tenterhooks, were suspended rows of bloaters and kippers that made your mouth water, just as they had been taken down from the smoke-house. You thought of those you knew living far away from the sea who would relish such a treat, popped inside, addressed two or three labels, and by the next post they were away, still with the delicious tang of oak smoke about them. Indeed, as you wandered round the back streets in those days you were always sniffing the smoke wafting out from innumerable small curing sheds, telling plainly enough that trade was flourishing. Not surprisingly, the town's footballers were called 'The Bloaters'.

The origin of this tasty morsel dates back to about 1835 when, so the story goes, a curer by the name of Bishop discovered at the end of the day a small quantity of fine fresh herrings which somehow or other had been overlooked. To avoid wasting them he applied a liberal sprinkling of salt, arranged them on spits and hung these where a batch of red-herrings was being smoked. Next morning he was pleasantly surprised at their golden appearance and even more so by their aroma and flavour when he came to taste them. Thereafter, he made a special point of producing 'bloaters'—so called because in the gentle heat they tend to bloat, or swell out—and as other curers began following his example they soon became popular.

The kipper first made its appearance about eight years later though it was not till 1846 that its inventor, John Woodger, sent his first consignment to London. It caught on immediately and was soon rivalling the Yarmouth bloater as a breakfast delicacy. Woodger did his first experiments in Newcastle using a very large chimney of the Elizabethan kind, so wide that he had no difficulty in hanging two or three hundred fish at a time. The hearth was proportionately big and able to burn oak logs or billets 7ft long. He may well have got the idea from the sides of home-cured bacon which in his time were commonly hung in chimneys to smoke over wood fires. First known as the 'Newcastle kipper' Woodger subsequently moved to Great Yarmouth, no doubt to make sure of regular supplies of prime, fresh herrings; after this the description 'Newcastle' was dropped and the single word kipper we use today was generally adopted.

The red-herring, or 'high-dried', is seldom seen these days, which is a pity for its rich, ham-like flavour was once greatly esteemed. It is a lengthy process to produce red-herring and this fact, rather than a change in tastes, has probably brought about its virtual disappearance. The herrings had to be salted and left for about three weeks when they were washed thoroughly in fresh water, spitted and hung in smoke for at least another three weeks. They were usually put right at the top of the smoke-house, hence the expression 'high-dried'. Beneath them, other herrings intended for bloaters, could be hung, smoked and taken down daily. A good bloater needs only light salting and a few hours in the smoke, the aim being to retain the essential flavour of the fresh fish together with the savour imparted by the smoke, which also extends the keeping time by two or three days. Ideally, it should be eaten soon after being taken out of the smoke-house and allowed to cool. The kipper usually gets a little longer in the salt and slightly more smoking but it, too, should not be left more than a day before eating. There are, of course, other kinds of fish besides herring which lend themselves to smoking and I shall discuss the different methods of preparing them in Chapter 9.

Many thousands of longshoremen gained a livelihood from the herring fisheries and although I have dealt mainly with the east coasts of Scotland and England there were many other areas where it was found in considerable numbers. The map which I have reproduced was drawn in the early 1930s and it shows that there was hardly any time during the year when it was not being caught in one place or another.

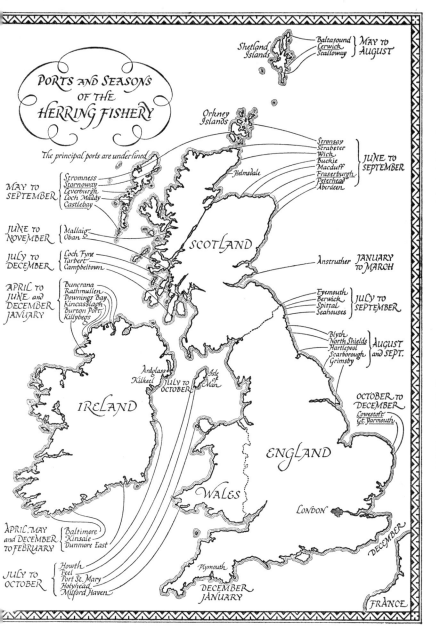

The location of herring shoals in the 1930s

I have had to use the past tense for much of what I have written above because the ruthless and indiscriminate pursuit of the herring has led to its virtual extermination. It is not my purpose to go into the controversial question of over-fishing but the sad decline of this once great fishery did not just happen like some unavoidable accident. Warnings of what might occur were being given as far back as the eighteenth century and ever since men of vision and imagination have seen clearly the rod we were making for our own backs. I will quote from one of them: 'When the Wick fishery first began (in the early 1800s) the fisherman could carry in a creel on his back the nets he required; now he needs a cart and a good strong horse!... I have always been slow to believe in the inexhaustibility of the shoals and can easily imagine the over-fishing, which some people pooh-pooh so glibly, to be quite possible . . . I maintain that the pitcher is going too often to the well—and that some day it will come back empty.'

That was written by J. G. Bertram in 1865. The pitcher is now coming back empty.

# CHAPTER FOUR

# Shoal Fish—2. Mackerel and Pilchards

Mackerel, like the herring, are fairly widely distributed; I have taken them from the deck of a battleship in Scapa Flow, spinning off north Norfolk beaches, drift-netting in the Solent and with feathers round Land's End. But it is mainly along the shores of southern England and off certain coasts of Ireland that we must look for any substantial fishery.

They make their first appearance during January in deep water to the south-west of the British Isles. The Cornishmen begin taking them in March and the season frequently extends well into the autumn. Very large catches used to be made during May, June and July in the English Channel, while tremendous quantities were once landed at Great Yarmouth and Lowestoft. A few are still to be had in the North Sea but they are no longer plentiful enough to warrant any large-scale operations.

Considerable shoals made their way into the Irish Sea between June and August and were followed by the Manx boats which at times drove a reasonably good trade. It was Kinsale, however, which grew into the chief centre of the Irish mackerel fishery, landings being made by local and Manx boats during March, April, May and June. On the west coast, Galway and Donegal Bay saw quite an important season from June to November.

The drift-net was used for mackerel as it was for herring, the only difference being a slightly larger mesh. Some fine boats were employed, the best known, perhaps, being the Cornish luggers. The illustration I have included gives a good idea of how they looked about the middle of last century; it comes from W. Brabazon's *Deep Sea and Coast Fisheries of Ireland*, published in 1848.

In the June 1878 issue of *The Field*, a contributor who had spent some time at sea in them, wrote as follows: 'They have long, easy lines; an almost perfectly balanced fore and aft body; no weight in the ends, no heavy bowsprit, boom or rigging; and not a large weight of ballast to carry. The mast, it is true, is stepped rather far forward, but the absence of a bowsprit more than compensates for this; whilst it may increase the momentum acquired during pitching and ascending, it does not cause them to plunge their bows under.' The fine sea-keeping qualities of these luggers were shown in 1854 when one of them, the *Mystery*, with seven hands, successfully completed the long haul to Melbourne, by way of the Cape, in 115 days.

A Cornish lugger of the 1840s

The larger vessels ranged from 40ft to 52ft but there was a smaller class measuring only about 30ft on the keel. They were open amidships with a small decking fore and aft. During the spring and early summer fishing off the south-west coast of Ireland many of these Cornish luggers made their headquarters at Kinsale where they were greatly admired by the local men. The Irish and Manx fishermen used very inferior boats little suited to the work they had to do. The majority that went drifting, for herring as well as mackerel, were cutter rigged, as in the illustration, and Brabazon emphasises the objections to this type of craft. 'Of the different rigs used by the boats employed at the herring fishery I consider the two best to be the dandy-rigged yawl and the lugger generally used by the St Ives men. If boats of these rigs can lower their main mast, as some of them can do, it gives them a great advantage while riding to their nets, as it prevents their rolling very considerably, they having no sail set at that time to steady them. Some herring boats are cutter rigged, which is very inconvenient as from their taunt [tall] mast, they roll so much that they are liable to shake the fish out of the net and even tear it in hauling it aboard.'

An Irish cutter-rigged drifter of the 1840s

Cornish luggers always lowered their foremast when lying to their nets and were provided with a variety of sails to meet all conditions of wind and weather. They seldom reefed as only one reef band was provided. When it was necessary to shorten sail the mizzen was shifted forward and a smaller one set aft; and this shifting went on until the small 'watch' mizzen (used when riding to the nets with foremast lowered) was reached. They usually carried the one large fore-lug and three mizzens, besides the watch mizzen.

While mackerel were caught in exactly the same way as herrings, their processing and disposal were quite different. Until fairly recent times they were neither cured nor smoked which meant they had to be brought to market and sold as quickly as possible. The mackerel is, perhaps, the most perishable of all fish and to be at its best should come straight out of the sea into the frying-pan. (A herring, by the way, is best caught today and eaten tomorrow.) The law, in its wisdom, took note of this and allowed mackerel to be cried through the streets on a Sunday.

Some Billingsgate salesmen, anxious to obtain them as fresh as possible, hired fast-sailing cutters to cruise in the Channel, collect catches from the men of Dover, Folkestone or Hastings, and speed back to London with every stitch they could carry. The south coast was just near enough to London to allow conveyance by road in vans, though this was much more expensive than by sea. Animals hauling fish vans were exempt from the post-horse duty but tolls had to be paid which were often quite heavy. Only the more valuable fish could be sent in this way, and just how valuable mackerel were we learn from W. Yarrell in his *History of British Fishes*, published in 1859. He records that in May 1807 the first load of Brighton mackerel sold for 40 guineas a hundred or 7 shillings each, reckoning six score to the hundred, a truly remarkable price bearing in mind the value of the pound 150 years ago. At Lowestoft, on 30 June 1831, the combined catches of sixteen boats sold for £5,252, or nearly £329 per boat. In early February 1834 a Hastings lugger sold her night's catch for more than £100. As further evidence of the immense quantities being caught at that time he mentions consignments sent from Rye to London on one night which exceeded 100 tons. At the height of the season as many as ten vans would be needed every day to take the Hastings catches to Billingsgate. If any remained they were put into the best-sailing lugger which made for the Thames and hailed a tug. Every hour was precious as 10,000 mackerel that might be worth £200 fresh would not make 20 shillings next day. So the outlay of £15–£20 for a tug was justified. By road, as by sea, there were hazards and not all the fish arrived safely at their destination. A consignment being sent from Portsmouth ended up in a Hampshire ditch when the coach it was travelling in, *The Star of Brunswick*, collided with a dog-cart near Horndean and overturned.

The usual procedure, after beaching the boats, was to arrange the catch in heaps on the sand where they were sold, generally to agents operating on behalf of London salesmen. It was done by 'Dutch auction'; one of the fishermen took charge and started by calling out a price well above the actual value, at the same time raising a large stone above his head with which 'to knock down' a

Beach auction of mackerel at Hastings

heap, or 'lot'. A quantity that might ultimately go for 40s would be offered at 60s, the seller rapidly naming a successively lower price until he got a taker, when the stone descended and the bidder became the purchaser. Such auctions were common wherever fish were landed in any quantity and the contemporary engravings I have included show two in progress. The first, dating from about 1835, depicts the scene as mackerel were being disposed of at Hastings, while the second, done in 1880, shows herrings being offered at Great Yarmouth. It will be noticed from the latter that the professional auctioneer has now made his

Beach auction of herrings at Great Yarmouth, about 1880

appearance, complete with top hat and bell-ringing assistant. On the right is another indication of impending change, the governess escorting her young charge who, spade in hand, is obviously taking a keen interest in the proceedings. It presages the shape of things to come, some ninety years later, when not a fish would be landed at Yarmouth and the whole town would be turned over to the tripper trade and the servicing of oil rigs.

In following the mackerel off the south coast English fishermen had frequently to contend with the none too friendly attentions of their opposite numbers from Boulogne and other French ports. These boats often had crews of eighteen or twenty men, whereas the English luggers carried less than half that number. So there was little they could do when the Frenchmen became aggressive, which happened all too often. They had no scruples about ordering English boats to leave areas if fish were plentiful and thought nothing of boarding them to see how successful they had been.

But no fracas with the French could compare with the bitter outburst of the Cornishmen against their fellows from the east coast in 1896. Up to a few years ago you might still have met old-timers in Cornwall, or in Norfolk and Suffolk, who remembered, or actually took part in, the Newlyn Riots. The trouble began on Sunday 17 May, when some Lowestoft boats started landing their catches, something they had done regularly for a great many years; in those days drifters from Great Yarmouth and Lowestoft used to spend sixteen weeks and more mackerel fishing in the neighbourhood of Mount's Bay and bringing their fish to Newlyn. The Cornishmen disapproved of fishing, or landing fish, on a Sunday (which to some extent they do to this day) and wished to stop the East Anglians from doing it. But the real cause of what happened was the very low price fish were making which week-end landings only aggravated.

It was apparent something unpleasant was afoot that Sunday evening when groups of people in pretty bad humour gathered round the harbour; but not till next morning did the storm burst when a crowd of Newlyn men, goaded on by jeering wives, surged over the quays, swept aside the small body of coastguards, boarded the east coast boats and flung a hundred thousand mackerel into the water. Many Lowestoftmen sought refuge by putting to sea, but the men of Newlyn quickly followed, boarded them, man-handled the crews, stove in water casks, slashed sails and threw everything they could lay hands on over the side. The *Bessie* suffered severely as did the *Boy Victor* which, on top of every-thing, lost all her cabin furniture. The sea was solid with dead fish wantonly cast overboard; the *Succeed* lost 13,000, the *Osprey* 7,000, the *Seraptah*, *Goodhope* and *Gallilean* 5,000 each, and the *Rosebud* 4,000. (See page 86.)

Encouraged by the local magistrates' unwillingness to read the Riot Act the Cornishmen next seized the portable wooden office of Hobson & Co, the Lowestoft buyers, and threw it into the harbour. On the Tuesday a company of 300 from Newlyn marched along the seafront to Penzance where several Lowestoft boats had put in. Here the police were more resolute; armed with batons and helped by a volunteer force of driftermen and dockworkers brandishing ice-axes, barrel staves and belaying pins, they met the advancing mob on the narrowest part of the quay. They laid about them to good effect with their improvised weapons and after a brief but bitter struggle beat back the attack.

Meanwhile, out in Mount's Bay, a sea battle was taking place. Two local luggers, towing gigs crammed with men, were determined on boarding the Lowestoft drifter *Maggie May*. Among her crew that day was Ernest Hovells, a youngster of 18, who half a century later retained very vivid memories of what took place. He lived in Hopton when I knew him twenty years ago and still did a bit of longshoring 'to keep his hand in'. 'Yes,' he used to say, 'that Newlyn business was a rum old do. The *Bessie* had taken all our fish on the Saturday to land at Newlyn (the *Maggie May* belonged to the same owner as had the *Bessie*, James Pye) so as we could go on fishing during the Sunday, and the Monday if need be. Well, by the time we did at last fetch Mount's Bay we knew for sure something was amiss, especially when we saw some of their luggers and small boats, all packed with men, making towards us. Our skipper could see right enough they meant mischief and without more ado told us to bring up a good supply of stones we carried for ballast. We didn't need telling twice and soon had piles of them ranged along the deck. All unsuspecting like the Cornishmen stood in to board us, but we waited till the distance was just right, and then we let fly.' Ernest would pause at this point, re-light his pipe with a spill and smile with undisguised satisfaction, remembering the discomfiture of the Cornishmen.

'In those days,' he would go on, 'I had a strong arm and could throw with the best of them. I saw my stones pitching into the nearest lugger and her people taking what scant cover they could, but we gave no quarter and kept on hulling our stones as if our life depended on it, as it might well have done. By this time I could see our skipper was bent on teaching them a proper lesson and hoisting all the sail we could, in between firing off our stones, we went about and made straight down to the Newlyners. The moment we got abreast of them over went a broadside, every man Jack at the rail, fair pelting those poor fellows. And it wasn't only stones they had you may be sure as each one was accompanied with some choice bits of language. By now they knew the game was up and ran back into harbour like scalded cats. In a little while we got a message to make for Plymouth and we arrived there without having lost a fish or had any damage done.'

It was not till the Thursday, after warships and troops had arrived, that order was restored and Newlyn returned to normal. An official enquiry was held soon after but surprisingly no proceedings were taken; two men only were bound over to come up for trial when called upon. Board of Trade arbitration assessed the damages for fish destroyed at the curiously precise sum of £619 15s 3d—to be divided among the owners, skippers and crews of the boats assaulted—but nothing was allowed for destruction of sails and gear. Fortunately, there was no recurrence of such scenes, the east and west coast men resuming their fishing without any show of hostility. Ernest Hovells summed it up when he said, 'I went to Newlyn many years after that but there was no trouble at all or any ill feeling'.

On the other side of the Atlantic an extensive mackerel fishery was carried on off the coasts of Maine and Massachusetts by the famous Gloucester schooners using dories and seine nets. The Americans developed a method of curing by cutting off the head, splitting down the back, removing the guts and rousing in Liverpool salt. Fish were then put into barrels which were topped up with brine. The fishing was very successful up to 1884 when 478,000 barrels were produced but after that it fell off disastrously and in 1890 the number was down to 19,000. This failure, which affected thousands of the poorer classes in New York, Boston and Philadelphia, led to supplies being sought overseas. Although things improved slightly during the next ten years the catch for 1900 amounted to no more than 23,000 barrels. In the meantime fish from Ireland, cured in the American style, helped to make up the deficiency and for many years this new trade gave a welcome boost to mackerel fishing here at home. Today, perhaps as a result of this American influence, pickled mackerel are readily obtainable in England and on the continent, while in their smoked form have recently become a popular, if rather expensive, delicacy.

Pilchards, the last of the shoal fish we are considering, formed a much more compact industry than mackerel; they were taken almost exclusively round the coasts of Cornwall and were salted immediately after capture, so there was no urgency about getting them to market. It was, perhaps, the most romantic and exciting

[Herring—*Clupea harengus.*]

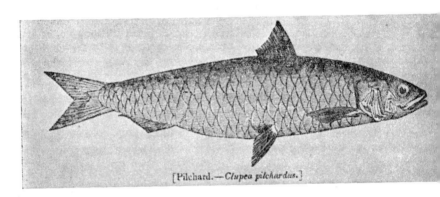

[Pilchard.—*Clupea pilchardus.*]

[The Mackerel.—*Scomber Scombrus.*]

The herring, pilchard and mackerel as depicted early last century

of all the fisheries as Wilkie Collins found when on a walking tour through Cornwall in the middle of last century. Setting down his experiences in a book which he called *Rambles Beyond Railways*, published in 1851, he wrote a most entertaining chapter on the Pilchard Fishery, and this is how he begins:

'If it so happened that a stranger in Cornwall went out to take his first walk along the cliffs towards the south of the county, in the month of August, that stranger could not advance far in any direction without witnessing what would strike him as a very singular and alarming phenomenon.

'He would see a man standing on the extreme edge of a precipice, just over the sea, gesticulating in a very remarkable manner, with a bush in his hand; waving it to the right and the left, brandishing it over his head, sweeping it past his feet—in short, apparently acting the part of a maniac of the most dangerous character. It would add considerably to the startling effect of this sight on the stranger if he were told, while beholding it, that the insane individual before him was paid for flourishing the bush at the rate of a guinea a week. And if he, thereupon, advanced a little to obtain a nearer view of the madman, and then observed on the sea below (as he certainly might) a well-manned boat, turning carefully to right and left exactly as the bush turned right and left, his mystification would probably be complete, and the time would arrive to come to his rescue with a few charitable explanatory words. He would then learn that the man with the bush was an important agent in the Pilchard Fishery of Cornwall; that he had just discovered a shoal of pilchards swimming towards the land; and that the men in the boat were guided by his gesticulations alone in securing the fish on which they and all their countrymen on the coast depend for a livelihood.'

This man was called a 'huer' and he may be seen 'on the extreme edge of a precipice, just over the sea' in the illustration taken from a print dated 1883 (see page 52). The boats, down in the bottom left-hand corner, are closing their net round a shoal over which sea birds are wheeling; meanwhile, the huer has obviously spotted another shoal further along the coast and is directing the nearest boats to it. This particular huer is using his sou'wester but a gorse branch with a piece of white linen tied round it was quite often employed as it showed up better.

Wilkie Collins saw for himself exactly how the fishing was carried on and I make no apologies for quoting his descriptions in detail. Having introduced the huer he turns to the fish themselves: 'The first sight from the cliffs of a shoal of pilchards advancing towards the land is not a little interesting. They produce on the sea the appearance of the shadow of a dark cloud. This shadow comes on and on until you can see the fish leaping and playing on the surface by thousands at a time, all huddled close together, and all approaching so near to the shore that they can be always caught in some fifty or sixty feet of water. Indeed, on certain occasions, when the shoals are of considerable magnitude, the fish behind have been known to force the fish before literally up to the beach, so that they could be taken in buckets, or even in the hand, with the greatest ease.'

Next, he goes on to record the actual method of capture: 'The principal boat used is at least fifteen tons in burden and carries a large net called the "seine" which measures a hundred and ninety fathoms in length and costs a hundred and seventy pounds—sometimes more. It is simply one long strip, from eleven to thirteen fathoms in depth, composed of very small meshes and furnished all along its length with lead at the bottom and corks at the top. The men who cast this net are called the "shooters" and receive eleven shillings and sixpence a week and a perquisite of one basket of fish each out of every haul.

'As soon as the huer discerns the first appearance of a shoal he waves his bush. The signal is conveyed to the beach immediately by men and boys watching near him. The seine net (accompanied by another small boat to assist in casting the net) is rowed out where he can see it. Then there is a pause, a hush of great expectation on all sides. Meanwhile, the pilchards press on—a great compact mass of thousands on thousands of fish, swimming to meet their doom. All eyes are fixed on the huer; he stands watchful and still until the shoal is thoroughly embayed in water which he knows to be within the depth of the seine net. Then, as the fish begin to pause in their progress and gradually crowd closer and closer together, he gives the signal; the boats come up and the net is cast, or in the technical phrase, shot overboard.

'The grand object is now to enclose the entire shoal. The leads sink the bottom to the ground, the corks keep the top to the surface of the water. When it has been taken all round the fish the two extremities are made fast and the shoal is then imprisoned within an oblong barrier of network surrounding it on all sides. The great art is to let as few of the pilchards escape as possible while this process is being completed. Whenever the huer observes from above that they are startled and are separating at any particular point, to that point he waves his bush, thither the boats are steered, and there the net is shot at once. In whatever direction the fish attempt to get out to sea they are thus immediately thwarted with extraordinary readiness and skill. This labour completed, the silence of intense expectation that has hitherto prevailed among the spectators on the cliff is broken. There is a great shout of joy on all sides—the shoal is secured!

'The seine is now regarded as a great reservoir of fish. It may remain in the water a week or more. To secure it against being moved from its position in case a gale should come on, it is warped by two or three ropes to points of land in the cliff and is at the same time contracted in circuit by its opposite ends being brought together and fastened tight over a length of several feet. While these operations are in course of performance another boat, another set of men, and another net (different in form from the seine) are approaching the scene of action.

'This new net is called the "tuck"; it is smaller than the seine inside which it is now to be let down for the purpose of bringing the fish closely collected to the surface. The men who manage this net are termed "regular seiners". They receive ten shillings a week and the same perquisite as the shooters. Their boat is first of all rowed inside the seine net and laid close to the seine boat, which remains stationary outside, and to the bows of which one rope at one end of the tuck net is fastened. The tuck boat then slowly makes the inner circuit of the seine, the smaller net being dropped overboard as she goes, and attached at intervals to the larger. To prevent the fish from getting between the two nets during this operation they are frightened into the middle of the enclosure by beating the water at proper places with oars and heavy stones fastened to ropes. When the tuck net has at length travelled round the whole circle of the seine and is securely fastened to the seine boat at the end as it was at the beginning, everything is ready for the great event of the day, the hauling of the fish to the surface.'

This tuck net, or 'tuck-seine' as it was often called, was 70 or 80 fathoms long and roughly 10 fathoms deep in the bunt, or centre. As it was hauled in the foot of the bunt was gradually raised so bringing the fish to the top, an operation that might have to be repeated several times if the shoal were a big one. But this first sight of the fish was greeted with tremendous enthusiasm as Wilkie Collins goes on to record: 'Now the scene on shore rises to a prodigious pitch of excitement. The merchants, to whom the boats and nets belong and by whom the men are employed, join the huer on the cliff. All their friends follow them; boys shout, dogs bark madly, every little boat in the place puts off crammed with idle spectators, old men and women hobble down to the beach to wait for news. The noise, the bustle and the agitation increase every moment. Soon the shrill cheering of the boys is joined by the deep voices of the seiners. There they stand, six or eight stalwart, sunburnt fellows, ranged in a row in the seine boat, hauling with all their might at the tuck net and roaring the regular nautical "Yo-heave-ho" in chorus. Higher and higher rises the net, louder and louder shout the boys and idlers. The merchant forgets his dignity and joins them; the huer so calm and collected hitherto, loses his self-possession and waves his cap triumphantly; even you and I, reader, uninitiated spectators though we are, catch the infection and cheer away with the rest as if our bread depended on the event of the next few minutes. "Hooray! Hooray! Yo-hoy, hoy, hoy! Pull away, boys! Up she comes! Here they are! Here they are!" The water boils and eddies; the tuck net rises to the surface and one teeming, convulsed mass of shining, glancing, silvery scales, one compact crowd of tens of thousands of fish, each one of which is madly endeavouring to escape, appears in an instant.

(*above*) Wick harbour, about 1860

*Page 85*

(*below*) Lassies gutting herrings at Aberdeen, about 1900

(*above*) Adversaries: West Country luggers of the kind which attacked East Anglian drifters during the Newlyn Riots of 1896

(*below*) The Lowestoft drifter *Hosanna*, similar to those set upon by the Cornishmen during the Newlyn Riots. In 1875 she lost 65 nets, cut by a Belgian trawler towing a 'devil'

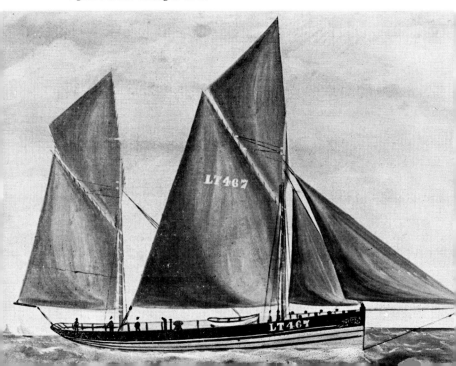

'The noise before was as nothing compared with the noise now. Boats as large as barges are pulled up in hot haste all round the net; baskets are produced by dozens; the fish are dipped up in them and shot out, like coals out of a sack, into the boats. Ere long, the men are up to their ankles in pilchards; they jump upon the rowing benches and work on until the boats are filled with fish as full as they will hold and the gunwales are within two or three inches of the water. Even yet the shoal is not exhausted; the tuck net must be let down again and left ready for a fresh haul while the boats are slowly propelled to the shore where we must join them without delay.

'As soon as the fish are brought to land one set of men, bearing capacious wooden shovels, jump in among them; and another set bring large hand-barrows close to the side of the boat into which the pilchards are thrown with amazing rapidity. This operation proceeds without ceasing for a moment. As soon as one barrow is ready to be carried to the salting-house another is waiting to be filled. When this labour is performed by night, which is often the case, the scene becomes doubly picturesque. The men with the shovels, standing up to their knees in pilchards, working energetically; the crowd stretching down from the salting-house, across the beach and hemming in the boat all round; the uninterrupted succession of men hurrying backwards and forwards with their barrows through a narrow way kept clear for them in the throng; the glare of the lanterns giving light to the workmen and throwing red flashes on the fish as they fly incessantly from the shovels over the side of the boat—all combine together to produce such a series of striking contrasts, such a moving picture of bustle and animation, as not even the most careless of spectators could ever forget.

'Having watched the progress of affairs on the shore we next proceed to the salting-house, a quadrangular structure of granite, well roofed in all round the sides but open to the sky in the middle. Here we must prepare ourselves to be bewildered by incessant confusion and noise; for here are assembled all the women and girls in the district piling up the pilchards on layers of salt, at threepence an hour; to which remuneration a glass of

F

brandy and a piece of bread and cheese are hospitably added at
every sixth hour by way of refreshment. It is a service of some
little hazard to enter this place at all. There are men rushing out
with empty barrows, and men rushing in with full barrows, in
almost perpetual succession. However, while we are waiting for
an opportunity to slip through the doorway we may amuse ourselves by watching a very curious ceremony which is constantly
in course of performance outside it.

'As the filled barrows are going into the salting-house we
observe a little urchin running by the side of them and hitting
their edges with a long cane in a constant succession of smart
strokes until they are fairly carried through the gate, when he
quickly returns to perform the same office for the next series that
arrive. The object of this apparently unaccountable proceeding is
soon practically illustrated by a group of children hovering about
the entrance of the salting-house who every now and then dash
resolutely up to the barrows and endeavour to seize on as many
fish as they can take away at one snatch. It is understood to be
their privilege to keep as many pilchards as they can get in this
way by their dexterity in spite of a liberal allowance of strokes
aimed at their hands; and their adroitness richly deserves its
reward. Vainly does the boy officially entrusted with the adminis-
tration of the cane strike the sides of the barrow with malignant
smartness and perseverance—fish are snatched away with lightning rapidity and pickpocket neatness of hand. The hardest rap
over the knuckles fails to daunt the sturdy little assailants. Howl-
ing with pain they dash up to the next barrow that passes them
with unimpaired resolution; and often collect their ten or a dozen
fish apiece in an hour or two. No description can do justice to the
"Jack-in-Office" importance of the boy with the cane as he
flourishes it about ferociously in the full enjoyment of his vested
right to castigate his companions as often as he can. As an instance
of the early development of the tyrannic tendencies of human
nature, it is, in a philosophical point of view, quite unique.

'But now, while we have a chance, while the doorway is
accidentally clear for a few moments, let us enter the salting-house
and approach the noisiest and most amusing of all the scenes

which the pilchard fishery presents. First of all we pass a great heap of fish lying in one recess inside the door, and an equally great heap of coarse, brownish salt lying in another. Then we advance further, get out of the way of everybody, behind a pillar, and see a whole congregation of the fair sex screaming, talking, and—to their honour be it spoken—working at the same time, round a compact mass of pilchards which their nimble hands have already built up to a height of three feet, a breadth of more than four, and a length of twenty. Here we have every variety of the "fairer half of creation" displayed before us, ranged round an odoriferous heap of salted fish. Here we can see crones of sixty and girls of sixteen; the ugly and the lean, the comely and the plump; the sour-tempered and the sweet—all squabbling, singing, jesting, lamenting and shrieking at the very top of their very shrill voices for "more fish" and "more salt"; both of which are brought from the stores, in small buckets, by a long train of children running backwards and forwards with unceasing activity and in bewildering confusion. But, universal as the uproar is, the work never flags; the hands move as fast as the tongues; there may be no silence and no discipline, but there is also no idleness and no delay. Never was threepence an hour more joyously or more fairly earned than it is here!

'The labour is thus performed. After the stone floor has been swept clean, a thin layer of salt is spread on it and covered with pilchards laid partly edgewise and close together. Then another layer of salt, smoothed fine with the palm of the hand, is laid over the pilchards; and then more pilchards are placed upon that; and so on until the heap rises to four feet or more. Nothing can exceed the ease, quickness and regularity with which this is done. Each woman works on her own small area without reference to her neighbour; a basketful of salt and a bucketful of fish being shot out into two little piles under her hands for her own special use. All proceed in their labour, however, with such equal diligence and equal skill that no irregularities appear in the various layers when they are finished—they run as straight and smooth from one end to the other as if they were constructed by machinery. The heap, when completed, looks like a long, solid, neatly-made mass of dirty salt; nothing being now seen of the pilchards but the extreme tips of their noses or tails, just peeping out in rows up the sides of the pile.'

That vivid and splendidly observed description by Wilkie Collins makes us wish that other distinguished writers had plied their pens to record the doings of longshoremen in their time of vigour. The historian of today must rely for the most part on 'accounts', 'statements' and 'observations', admirable of their kind but failing to breathe any spark of life into their subjects or give the feel and flavour of toil that was so often unique, always arduous and but rarely rewarding in terms of wealth or comfort. Only incidentally do we learn of hazards occasioned by bad weather, of poor boats and gear the concomitant of poverty, of predatory middlemen, of shoals that failed to appear and once-productive grounds fish unaccountably forsook. Wilkie Collins gives us a complete picture in glowing tones and what he did not actually see for himself he was at pains to learn about from the best of all possible sources, an ancient fisherman:

'What more remains to be done,' he concludes, 'will not be completed until after an interval of several weeks. We must be content to hear about this from information given to us by others. Yonder, sitting against the outside wall of the salting-house, is an intelligent old man, too infirm now to do more than take care of the baby that he holds in his arms while the baby's mother is earning her threepence an hour inside. To this ancient we will address all our enquiries; and he is well qualified to answer us for the poor old fellow has worked away all the pith and marrow of his life in the pilchard fishery.

'The fish—as we learn from our old friend who is mightily pleased to be asked for information—will remain in salt or, as the technical expression is, "in bulk", for five or six weeks. During this period a quantity of oil, salt and water drips from them into wells cut in the centre of the stone floor on which they are placed. After the oil has been collected and clarified it will sell for enough to pay off the whole expense of the wages, food and drink given to the seiners—perhaps defraying other incidental charges besides. The salt and water left behind, and offal of all sorts found with it, furnish a valuable manure. Nothing in the pilchard itself, or in connection with the pilchard, runs to waste—the precious little fish is a treasure in every part of him.

'After the pilchards have been taken out of "bulk", they are washed clean in salt water and packed in hogsheads which are then sent for exportation to some large sea-port—Penzance for instance—in coast traders. The fish reserved for use in Cornwall are generally cured by those who purchase them. The export trade is confined to the shores of the Mediterranean—Italy and Spain providing the two great foreign markets for pilchards.'

The dependence of the Cornish people on Catholic countries to buy the *firmados*, or salted pilchards, is neatly summed up in the following toast:

> 'Here's a health to the Pope! May he live to repent
> And lengthen by six months the term of his Lent;
> And tell all his vassals who value their souls,
> There's nothing like *Pilchards* for saving their souls!'

Besides seining, drift-netting was carried on but only to a limited extent as less than a sixth of the catches were taken in this way. The odd boat may still be found throwing a few nets into the sea and during the autumn months Cornish fish shops occasionally have small quantities for sale. Otherwise the glory has departed; seining and salting are things of the past and with them have gone not only the tumult and the shouting but a whole way of life.

Had the pilchard been as versatile as the herring there is little doubt the industry would have grown and prospered more. But it cannot be bloatered or kippered for when spitted and hung breaks its neck as soon as the fires are lit; and being full of oil catches alight the moment it reaches the flames when like as not the smoke-house will be burned down. This danger was well known to the fisher girls on the east coast which is why, on the rare occasions when a stray pilchard was found among the herrings, it was at once seized and impaled on the lintel of the smoke-house door, 'to drive away others that might be swimming with the herrings'.

The method of salting, although suited to the foreign palate, found little favour with the English and the home demand for cured pilchards was therefore negligible. Being the same fish as the sardine, some effort was made a hundred years ago to preserve them in oil and market them in those familiar tins which usually have a French or Portuguese label. But no capital was available for the project and it petered out.

The fresh sardines of France deliciously fried in butter and served with tiny new potatoes could find their counterpart in Cornwall if hotels and restaurants made use of their locally caught pilchards; what a change they would make from the tired fillets of white fish which have struggled down from Aberdeen or Grimsby and lie sadly on the plate with an oily mass of sodden chips. Years ago the Cornish housewife had her own special method of cooking fresh pilchards which she called 'scrowling'. The head was left on but the fish was split right down the belly and the guts removed; the insides were then generously sprinkled with pepper, two fish were put together, backs outside, and the pair roasted on a grid-iron till they were just tender. They also lend themselves to 'sousing' in the same way as herrings and mackerel. A Bridport fisherman's wife once told me her simple method: 'Boil them or steam them,' she said, 'for about three minutes to soften them a little, then soak them in vinegar. If you like you can simmer them gently in the vinegar with a few bay leaves sprinkled on top, but let them get cold before eating them.'

Such were the great shoal fisheries which for centuries kept thousands of men employed on our coasts, added considerably to our export trade and, perhaps most important of all, provided an abundance of cheap, fresh and wholesome food for rich and poor alike. Nets were used for their capture because no other method could have taken them in such numbers. But for some fish, especially where the bottom is rough or rocky, the net is useless and recourse must be had to the hook. That is the subject of the next chapter.

# CHAPTER FIVE

# Hookers

With a hook, a length of line and some bait, man, as we have seen, has been hauling in fish for his needs from the rivers, estuaries and seas at least since Old Testament times and probably for much longer. It is a simple, cheap and effective method which has survived, though on an ever diminishing scale, down to the present day.

Commercial fishermen are not prone to regard their calling as a sporting contest, yet I have often noticed a quickening of excitement, an added zest, when boats are engaged in lining. There is an element of personal combat, a kind of gladiatorial feeling as the fish, especially if it be a large one, is hauled up, gaffed and dropped on the deck. With drift-nets the fish are gilled, drowned and dead long before they get to the boat's side; most are dead, too, when released from the cod-end of a trawl. In a way you feel they have given themselves up; but you can never be sure of a hooked fish until it is lying safely on deck or flapping about on the bottom boards.

There are exceptions, of course; most fish taken by hook in very deep water, for instance, are generally dead or dying when brought to the surface. I recall a day spent groper fishing in Cook Strait, New Zealand, with some Italian immigrant longshoremen who were working grounds 90 fathoms deep, when every one of the great fish was dead by the time we got it on board. The occasional shark seemed better able to withstand the change of pressure and needed careful handling before it could be despatched. This was about the only excitement that came to enliven the otherwise monotonous work of unhooking the lifeless groper, heading and gutting them, and shovelling the refuse over the side.

The only excitement, that is, until flocks of sea birds began gathering round, just as they do in northern waters, when I was thrilled to see two Royal albatrosses wheeling lazily overhead and inspecting the tasty morsels streaming away from us on the tide. A number of mollymawks, cape pigeons, small petrels and handsome southern black-backed gulls had already alighted and were tucking into the feast; I knew albatrosses to be surface feeders also and asked the skipper if they were likely to come down.

In that Italo–New Zealand drawl which delighted me all the time I had been on board, he replied: 'Yees, I theenk they weel. Some time they do, but land long way away, then swim very slow to boat. We kind to them, give them fish feed, so not afraid to come close.'

'You mean they'll actually come alongside?'

'Yees, p'r'haps so. But after they land, take no notice, be busy in boat, then they get bold.'

We both looked up, so did the rest of the crew. The slow, majestic circling of the two great birds continued without a movement of the wings, the fresh, southerly wind and a span of some 10ft giving all the lift they needed to glide sedately while deciding if they should look in on us for lunch.

For five minutes they held our gaze when the skipper said quietly, obviously as impressed as I with the beauty of their soaring flight: 'See, they make up their minds, they come lower now. I theenk they join us, yees?'

And in no time at all it seemed they had lost height and were planing down dead into the eye of the wind about a hundred yards from the boat. We could see clearly their legs stretched out as they neared the water and the great webbed feet inclined at an angle of 45 degrees to the surface. Then they touched, there was a scatter of spray, the wings slowly arched up to spill the wind, the white breast feathers mingled with the spray which disappeared almost at once as they came to rest. Satisfied that all was well the wings were flexed once or twice then neatly folded away and without the slightest show of hurry or urgency they began paddling towards us.

'Beautiful theengs they are really,' said the skipper, smiling his appreciation, 'always make me think of flying-boats landing in the sea when I was a boy.' And a more apt description I cannot think of.

He went to one of the bait boxes and took a couple of fish, rather like our horse-mackerel only bigger, which he filleted then cut in strips about an inch wide, remarking as he did so that albatrosses would not look at the guts and trimmings we were putting over the side but would only take the flesh. The main diet of an albatross consists of surface-swimming fish and squid, which latter are sought mainly at night when they, too, have the habit of coming to the surface. But having no squid the skipper began tempting them with the strips he had prepared, throwing three or four of them up tide and towards the two birds which had now paddled within twenty yards of us.

We moved about the deck pretending to take no notice but keeping an eye lifted all the time to see if they would accept our offerings. To our delight they did. Moving quite fast now they made straight for them and with a quick jab of the beak each piece was seized, sampled, approved of and swallowed.

'You very hungry birds today, I theenk,' said the skipper, tipping me a wink and picking up several more strips which he had laid along the rail. With the merest flick of his wrist he threw two of them no more than ten feet from the boat's side, then stayed absolutely still. I did the same partly concealed by some boxes stacked against the wheelhouse. Then, quite fearlessly, they came on till they were little more than a fathom away, took the fish and remained quite still looking up at us. The larger of the two I christened in my mind Oliver Twist.

'He wants some more!' I whispered to the skipper, as softly as I could, but before the words were spoken I saw that he had somehow contrived to pass a strip to the hand that was over the side and was dangling it not three feet from the big fellow. I watched, fascinated. Would that immense, wild creature really feed from the skipper's hand? The bird looked at the man, the man looked at the bird, and perhaps in that meeting of eyes was born the confidence which allowed the one to raise his gift an inch or two above the water and the other to put forth his neck and take the gift into his beak. For that is what happened; for a brief instant both bird and man had hold of the same scrap of fish till the one let go and the other stared back his thanks.

The whole crew had stopped work completely absorbed by this strange, and to all of us, quite wonderful encounter.

'That bird, I theenk, he know another old sailor when he see one,' murmured the mate, nodding his head.

'How so?' I asked, a bit mystified.

'You know what they say, don't you?' he answered, not raising his voice but all the time gazing steadfastly at his skipper and the albatross, 'all albatross really the souls of old sailors who have passed on. Sometime they like come back, just see how we young sailors get along. Them birds they don't forget their sailor days.'

Fancy? Of course! Yet he had reminded me of Lowestoft and the flocks of well-fed gulls which forever haunted the fish market, proud, imperious looking, cast in much the same mould as these albatrosses, wild creatures, too, whose home was the grey North Sea. They trod the quays and searched for offal in the harbour because it was an easy way to find a breakfast, lunch or tea. 'But 'taint all they come for, boy,' said a grey-bearded old smacksman to me once, many years ago, 'an' do yew disbelieve them what tell yew 'tis.' Three splendid black-backed gulls were preening themselves on bollards not five paces away as he spoke, the white of their breasts sparkling like new-fallen snow, the black top sides of their wings glinting like Whitby jet. He saw me admiring them and smiled. Then I summoned up courage to ask what it was they came for if it wasn't food. 'What do they come for?' he repeated, 'why, boy, jest t' see the likes o' we old fishermen, 'cos not long ago they were our shipmates, so that's why they come by here, to keep a sort of eye on us.' He must be having me on, I thought to myself, yet he looked serious enough and I felt it was no place for a stripling like I to doubt his words. Eventually I managed to blurt out that it didn't seem possible to be shipmates with birds, so what did he mean? 'A-a-h, well, boy, it be this way. Now an' agin fishin' can be dangerous work, 'specially in bad weather, an' men get washed overboard and drownded. Like as not yew never see 'em again, but their souls, boy, their souls fly into the nearest gull that's floating around. An' then, when th' boat runs back to port, them birds follow, an' here they stay, jest as I told yew, to keep an eye on their old shipmates.'

I saw the skipper motioning to me to pick up a piece of fish and join him by the rail. 'I theenk,' he murmured, so quietly I had to strain my ears to hear what he was saying, 'if you hold the feesh now, instead of me, that big chap he come and eat from you. Try and see.'

No more than three feet away from my hand the two birds were stemming the tide with gentle movements of their webbed feet; I dangled the fish on the surface and felt my heart thumping with excitement as I came face to face with them for the first time. Would they, I wondered, feel the same confidence in me they had in the skipper? Could I engender the same trust?

They were close together now peering intently at the proffered fish. I noticed their eyes, sparkling like crystals in the brilliant light thrown up by the sea; the unbelievable whiteness of head, throat and breast setting off the burnished black of the wings; above all, the large and powerful beak, of a soft yellow hue, with the upper mandible curving over the end of the lower, perfectly adapted for taking food on, or just below, the surface.

Once paired albatrosses remain with the same mate for life, which some ornithologists believe may span forty or fifty years. I felt sure these two must be a pair but it was hard to say how old they were. But as they spend the first five or six years of their lives entirely at sea, coming to the land at the end of that time to form a pair bond, but not to breed, which only commences about the ninth or tenth year, and as this was the middle of the breeding season, when one or other should have been occupied at the nest, I estimated they were between six and nine years old and had so far not reared any young. Their spotless, unruffled plumage tended to confirm this.

Neither bird had made a move to take my fish as if aware it was being offered by a strange hand; nor did they retreat. So, copying what the skipper had done, I slowly stretched out my arm towards them when, to my sheer delight, the hen paddled closer, extended her neck and with a quick dart of her beak took tight hold of the fish. I remember giving my end a slight tug just to make sure she really had it, then I let go; a sharp upward jerk of the head followed, she half-opened her beak, swallowed once, then again, and it was gone. I had actually succeeded in hand-feeding an albatross!

'It's what I say', argued the mate, with the skipper and the rest of the crew, 'them birds, they know old sailors all right,' which might possibly have referred to me but was, I think, intended more as a compliment to the bird. For the next half hour or so we got on with the job of heading and gutting groper, many a prime piece going over the side that should rightly have ended up on the fishmongers' slabs. At last, when they could obviously eat no more, the two albatrosses pointed south into the wind, spread their enormous wings and, with a running motion of their feet over the surface, took off into the cloudless sky. They circled once high above us—'They're saying thank-you, I theenk,' said the skipper, happily—and in a couple of minutes had disappeared.

Hooks are used in a variety of ways according to conditions and the kinds of fish to be taken. The most common method is to set lines with hooks spaced about a fathom apart which are kept lying on the sea-bed with stones, lead weights or small anchors. They are called ground lines and as the name implies are meant to catch bottom-feeding fish such as plaice, brill, turbot and flounders besides whiting, haddock, cod, ling, gurnards and conger eels. In fact there is hardly any kind of fish which at one time or another you don't catch when lining. I remember throwing a line with six small hooks into Southampton Water during the war and using freshly dug lug-worm for bait had great hopes of getting a flounder or an eel. But after two hours without a bite and the drizzle turning into a steady rain I decided to call it a day. Hauling in for the last time I found I had two surprising captures, a very fine oyster and a 4lb skate.

Finding enough bait of the right kind has always been a problem for line fishermen; to be more accurate it was the wives and children who had the problem because it fell to them to hunt for it while the menfolk were off in the boats. Whelks, particularly for the cod fishing, mussels and clams were what they went after; but having returned with full baskets their work was not finished as they then had to turn to and bait the lines ready for next day. Deep-sea boats would often shoot five or six miles of lines, called great lines, requiring bait for some 5,000 hooks and by the early 1900s the cost of this could easily run to £10 if it had to be bought; nowadays it would be nearer £100. The so-called long lines of the inshore men seldom exceeded a mile in length but it was hard enough work preparing even such short lines especially if bait were scarce. Great lines are now virtually things of the past but long lining is still carried on in quite a few areas.

In the above methods, which differ only in the length of line and number of hooks shot, the fish catch themselves so to speak, while the boat waits at anchor or returns to port, not hauling the catch till evening or perhaps next day. Another, and once very important, way of using the hook was in hand lining. Each member of the crew had a line long enough to reach to the bottom with a substantial lead weight attached and usually three hooks. The boat could be at anchor or moving slowly under easy sail and when fish were plentiful enormous quantities were caught. The great virtue of this method was that every fish came up alive and kicking and this was how the well-smacks, already referred to, obtained their catches. Each was carefully unhooked to cause the minimum of injury and put immediately into the well through which sea water was continually circulating; once full the smack made all sail for port where the catch was transferred to chests, perforated containers floating in the docks, where it could remain, often for several weeks without any serious deterioration, until required for market. Those who visited Denmark before the war may recall the Copenhagen fish-market where women in national costume drove a useful trade ladling out live 'red-spotters', or plaice, from the tanks around them, heading, gutting and filleting them while you waited: somewhat barbarous I always thought it but at least you got fresh fish.

November to February was the great cod season in the North Sea, the two most important grounds being on the Dogger Bank and Cromer Knoll. Large, mature fish came from these areas and were the ones taken to Grimsby and Harwich for retention in chests. These measured 7ft in length, 4ft in width and were 2ft deep. Battens at the bottom and planks along the sides, placed slightly apart from each other, allowed the water to circulate freely, but the top was boarded over, except for a trap door through which the fish were put in and taken out. A chest could hold about forty mature fish or nearly a hundred smaller ones. Only cod, and occasionally haddocks, could be preserved in this way, the close confinement being fatal for most other kinds. In 1872 there were no less than 400 of these chests in use at Grimsby making it possible to have in store from 15,000 to 20,000 live cod.

E. W. H. Holdsworth, whose *Deep-Sea Fishing and Fishing Boats*, published in 1874, was soon to be regarded as the most authoritative work of its kind, gives a lively account of what went on when a supply of these fish was required: 'A remarkable scene is presented, and one peculiar to Grimsby and Harwich, the places where live cod are kept in store. It is well known that as a rule fish are firmer and better for the table if they are killed as soon as taken out of the water, instead of being allowed to die slowly by suffocation as the gills become dry and incapable of performing their proper function. This is especially the case with cod; and as a matter of humanity it may be a question whether there is much to choose between the sudden and violent death to which they have now to submit and the slower and, it may be called, more natural process of dying from want of water. The interests of the fish dealers and the gastronomic taste of the consumers have, however, settled the question in favour of violence; and the proceeding no doubt derives a great deal of its appearance of inhumanity from being conducted on a large scale, as at Grimsby, where hundreds of fish are sometimes killed in the course of a day.

'When the time arrives for preparing the fish for market a chest of cod is brought alongside a hulk kept for the purpose and moored in the dock near the market-place. Tackles from a couple of davits are then hooked on to the handles and the chest is hoisted up till nearly clear of the water which drains through the bottom and leaves the fish dry. The cover is then taken off and a man gets into the opening and takes out the fish, seizing them by the head and tail. The commotion among perhaps forty or fifty cod just out of the water is of course very great and it is often no easy matter to get a good hold of them; but, one after the other, they are lifted out and thrown up to the deck of the hulk, where they are taken in hand by another man, who performs the duties of executioner. He grasps the fish tightly behind the head with his left hand, holds it firmly on the deck, and giving a few heavy blows on the nose with a short bludgeon, kills it at once. With a large and lively fish it is sometimes as much as can be done to hold it down with one hand on the slippery deck whilst giving it the *coup de grace*; but the work is generally skilfully performed and the dead fish rapidly accumulate into a large heap whence they are taken on shore to be packed in bulk in the railway trucks waiting close by to receive them. Each truck will hold about twelve score of good-sized fish, or a proportionately larger number of smaller ones. The fish thus killed and packed reach Billingsgate in time for the market early next morning and are known in the trade by the name of "live cod"... they command the highest price and are looked upon as essentially "West End" fish.

'The advantage of being able to store the cod alive is of course a general one; for not only is the market more regularly supplied than would otherwise be the case, owing to small catches during bad weather or delays from calms or adverse winds, but the fish themselves come into the hands of the fishmongers in a fresher state than almost any other kinds supplied to them.'

It was the introduction of the well-smacks and the need to preserve their catches alive for as long as possible after reaching port that led to the development of such methods of storage. Eventually such smacks were abandoned and new ones were built which put to sea with plentiful supplies of ice which kept the dead fish in good state till they returned to port; then more ice in the railway trucks and vans ensured their arrival at market without too much deterioration. Nowadays, ice has given place to refrigerated containers which makes possible the eating of a sole in New Caledonia six months or a year after it was caught in the English Channel; that it tastes less like fish than a piece of salted blotting-paper is, perhaps, immaterial as 'the gastronomic taste of the consumers' mentioned by Holdsworth no longer has any commercial application. With shrinking supplies, alternatives being dredged up from ever more distant waters and a frightening, never ceasing increase in the number of mouths to be fed, quality has, inevitably, gone by the board. For those who still seek it the only advice I can give, so far as fish is concerned, is to go out and catch it.

The idea of keeping fish alive in well-boats probably originated in Holland. The first English vessels of this kind were built at Harwich in 1712. There were three of them, based on the Dutch model, and they proved so successful that nine more were launched between 1715 and 1720. By 1735 their numbers had

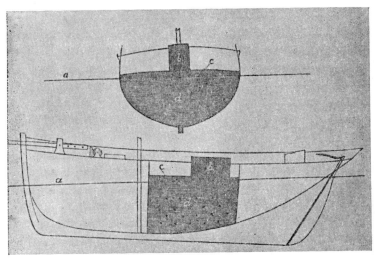

A well boat. The entrance to the well was through a hatchway (b). Forward, and on each side of it, ran the 'well-deck' (c) which kept the level of the water (a) within certain limits when the vessel was rolling or pressed down under sail

increased to thirty. War with France in 1744 led to many being laid up or sold but with the return of peace in 1748 the fleet grew till it numbered thirty-seven. Further interruption occurred during the seven years of war from 1756 to 1763 but afterwards more and more vessels were built till by 1778 no less than seventy-three

(*above*) *Silver Spray II* mackerel lining off Land's End

*Page 103*

(*below*) Using feathers when a shoal has been struck; there is often a fish on every hook

(*above*) Sizing the catch

(*below*) Shooting a seine net

sail were working out of Harwich, of from 45–55 tons burden. During this next period of hostilities a French privateer, in one day, captured thirteen Harwich boats on the Dogger Bank, which so incensed the Essex fishermen who claimed the navy gave them no protection, that they laid up their boats and stayed ashore.

Following this episode, strange as it may seem, two French gentlemen arrived from Dieppe bearing an assurance from their government that all privateers had received strict orders not to interfere in any way with English fishing boats. Accordingly the Harwich men fitted out and once more put to sea grateful for the consideration shown them by the French. Unfortunately, however, our own privateers seem to have been given no similar instructions and soon after carried off five French fishing vessels which they claimed as prizes. Thereupon the Harwich and Thames fishermen held a meeting and undertook to send the value of these boats to France by way of compensation, no mean gesture considering that Harwich alone had to provide 350 guineas and the Thames estuary men, mostly from Greenwich, 150 guineas.

Fishing now continued without further molestation till 1780 when Holland came into the war and Dutch privateers got busy, especially off the Norfolk coast, on one occasion capturing no less than fifteen sail. Getting little or no protection from British warships the Harwich boats were either laid up or offered for sale. Then the Norwegians appeared on the scene offering to buy the Harwich boats, the aim being, so it was alleged, to cripple the Essex men's trade, particularly in lobsters which, like cod, were kept alive in welled vessels. Many were disposed of in this way but at only about half their real value. When war began again with France in 1793 few fishermen were willing to put to sea and supplies to the London market grew less and less. In 1810 the government offered bounties 'for taking and bringing fish to the cities of London and Westminster and other places in the United Kingdom', but it was an artificial method of trying to boost supplies, born of desperation, and did little good. Following Waterloo and with only natural hazards to be encountered on the North Sea fishermen needed no prodding from the state to get on

G

with their job. So, during their first hundred years, the well-boats of Harwich had quite an exciting history; but they survived and continued in use for another half century or so when they were gradually replaced by vessels carrying ice to preserve their catches.

The cod chests at Grimsby were square shaped so that they could be moored together and take up the minimum of room. The Leigh men, however, used a quite different shape as they took their chests to sea, towed astern of their pinks, peter-boats or bawleys, and filled them up with the fish caught. They were called 'koffs' and because they bore some slight resemblance to a coffin this has been thought by some to be the origin of the name. More likely, however, it derives from the Dutch and German 'koffer', a chest or trunk. A 'vishen koffer' in Dutch is simply a fish box.

The Leigh koff was made of deal boards half an inch thick, was 9ft long, $2\frac{1}{2}$ft broad and about 10in deep. The forward part was wedge shaped, the stern square with only a slight tendency to a counter. The sides and bottom were pierced with a multitude of holes 1in in diameter. The top had a large, square opening with a lid easily fastened by staple and wooden plug or padlock. The bow was fitted with a ringbolt through which a rope was spliced with a thimble and with this the koff was towed.

It is rather surprising that with the success of well-boats at Grimsby and Harwich other areas should have taken so long in adopting them. When hooks and lines provided so much of the fish landed and keeping them alive was the surest way of getting them to market in the freshest possible state, it can only be put down to the proverbial conservatism of fishermen that they were not more speedily accepted on other parts of the coast. From James Murie, already quoted, we learn that 'it was about 1790 or even later before the middle Thames fishermen at Gravesend, Greenwich and Barking took to the welled smacks. The introduction of welled boats at Leigh is not recorded but the very oldest fishermen say their parents recall the little pink sterns as possessing small wells somewhat similar in pattern to the afterwards larger welled bawleys.' He goes on to say that by 1898, the time when he was writing, there were only six or eight well-boats left at Leigh. So in the Thames estuary they would seem to have had only a limited span of usefulness, probably due to the quickness with which catches could be despatched to Billingsgate.

The potential value of this and other English markets was recognised in Ireland as early as 1736 when one, William Doyle, hydrographer, discovered the Nymph Bank off the south coast, so named after the vessel in which he was surveying, but it was not till early in the nineteenth century that a company was formed to fish there and send catches to London in well-boats. Robert Fraser was the instigator and in 1818 he published *A Review of the Domestic Fisheries of Great Britain and Ireland* which contains much valuable information about the state of the fishing industry at that time.

He went himself to the Nymph Bank and found an abundance of cod, turbot, plaice, skate and soles which encouraged him to start a company that could supply places like Liverpool and Bristol as well as London. Two vessels were purchased, the *Phoenix* and the *Mary*, but it appears there was internal dissension which prevented the scheme being given a fair trial though he records that the *Phoenix* did make one passage to London. It took her 4 days 11hr and she carried 35 score of live cod and 66 score of salted.

The formation of another company was proposed in 1854 to be known as The London and West of Ireland Fishing Company, sponsored by a retired naval commander, Thomas Edward Symonds. He, too, put pen to paper and a year later published *Observations on the Fisheries of the West Coast of Ireland,* a very readable study which shows how thoroughly he had gone into the matter. Despite the absence of any real effort to fish these waters by the natives, strenuous efforts were made to keep out or limit the foreigner. In Elizabeth's reign, says Symonds, vessels from other countries were prohibited from fishing in Irish waters without a licence, the cost of which was 13s 4d for every twelve tons the vessel could carry. Philip II of Spain had to pay the Irish treasury £1,000 to fish there, while Charles I exacted from the Dutch no less a sum than £30,000 to establish a fishing station on the island of Ennis Boffin, off the Mayo coast. In Symonds' day many of their descendants were still to be found there. In 1650, however, there was a remarkably generous dispensation when Sweden was allowed to employ 100 vessels in the Irish fisheries without any payment at all.

About 1800 some American boats came to Ireland and were allowed to fish experimentally for three years. Results were promising and they offered, subject to the approval of the British government, to create a fishing establishment and invest £100,000 in it. This seemingly handsome proposal was turned down, though for what reasons I do not know. Thereafter it was left to the Irish, with the help of some Manx and English boats, to make what they could of their own waters.

They ought to have made a great deal as Symonds shows. Like all good company promoters he was at pains to put before possible subscribers as full an account as he could of the information on which he based his proposals, and to that end sought the advice of several individuals already closely involved with the fishing. In doing so he unwittingly provides us with a complete picture of how the Irish fishery was conducted a century and a quarter ago as well as evidence of the superabundance of all kinds of fish which then existed.

'Being desirous of getting a practical opinion on the details of any proposed arrangements,' Symonds writes, 'as well as to test the accuracy of my own impressions in favour of Galway as a fishing station, I put myself in communication with a gentleman who has conducted a fishing establishment on the coast for the last four years... On acquainting him with my views, and requesting his opinion on the resources of that part of the coast, he sent me the following practical and deeply interesting letter, which, as it bears materially on the subject of supply, I here introduce:

Fishing Office, Galway,<br>May 29th, 1855.

My Dear Sir,

    I shall give you an outline of the resources of the west coast of Ireland, from Galway Bay to Erris Head, north, and north-west to Donegal Bay. From the month of November to 17th March cod-fish are in their primest season. In-shore ling fishing begins in January and ends in April, but the most profitable, on account of the quantity taken, is fishing in June, July and August; same season for congers, cod, skate, &c. Hake fishing begins in June and ends in November in Galway Bay, during which period we commonly take from five hundred to one thousand in a haul of five to six hours in the trawl-net; prime haddock in spring, chiefly off Boffin Island, but they frequently fall into this bay in large quantities. Large mackerel are driven into Arran (thirty miles off) in spring by the sun-fish (or basking shark); but in July this bay swarms with smaller mackerel and all kinds of small fish, which could be cured for export or readily sold here. Immense quantities might be taken with large seine or drift-nets. Sun fish are worth about £40 each (that is, the *livers*, which weigh about thirty cwt. – the carcase is cast off as useless); they come along the whole coast in large shoals and in fine weather are easily harpooned. The oil ranks in value next to sperm and is used for lamps; this year it was sold at 4s 6d. per gallon in Galway; it was not well prepared being boiled in common pots. Herrings are in the bay now, but the fishermen's nets are not deep enough to fish where they are; they will not come into shallow water till August. The winter herring fishing is far the most valuable on this coast; they are very large and fine fish and will sell in England and Dublin, &c., at 6s. to 7s. per hundred for bloating. Fourteen Killybegs herrings in full season will weigh one stone. Sprat fishing is valuable from the quantity of oil they contain, used by tanners; after expressing the oil, the fish are eagerly bought in winter for consumption by the poor, which pays first cost. Coal-fish is largely taken here; they are very productive in oil and the dry fish meets with a ready sale.

Trawling in this bay and coast will pay well all the year round, as turbot, sole, brill, plaice, &c., never leave the coast, and owing to railway transit arrive in good order at market. *I only missed one week's trawling from bad weather since July last.* The offal, of course, would be very considerable from a good fleet of boats; the refuse of the fish-market can be purchased at 3d. per cwt.

Besides, there are banks of shell-fish – mussels (bank dry at spring tides), scallops, &c., when any number of tons could be taken with a dredge in 7 to 10 fathoms of water. Indeed, we often avoid the bank, though lots of turbot, &c., are on it, as the trawls get torn with the weight of scallops in them; so with a dredge what may not be taken? Mussels may be contracted for in Galway at 2s. or so per ton. There are also many unworked, or imperfectly worked, salmon fisheries in Connemara and Mayo where fish could be bought cheap or the fisheries rented. I supplied nets last year at one-third of the fish free, and bought the other two-thirds at 3d. per lb. (salmon), white trout 2½d. per lb., and this year can fish on same terms. I am quite sure a very large supply of salmon may be had by making arrangements in time next year.

The lobster fishing is only prosecuted by poor men (who contract with small dealers). Their boats are small, from 2 to 4 tons. They only fish from Boffin to Achill (for Dublin market), and as they must return once or twice a week they cannot go far, nor can they bring their lobsters in good condition to market, particularly as they all peg them; but were a proper method introduced, and suitable well-boats to attend and purchase, also to fish, the quantity taken would be almost incredible. They are the finest lobsters I ever saw, particularly Boffin Achill, Black Rock, Stags of Broadhaven, &c., &c.; also the whole coast of Donegal. The Connemara turf boats alone bring into Galway two or three hundred dozen per week in summer time, and were proper means adopted to keep them till wanted an enormous supply could be obtained; in fact, there would be no occasion to go to Norway for lobsters.

There is not an island, inlet, creek nor rock on the whole north-west coast that does not abound with shell-fish. Crabs are thrown away as useless. Shell-fish, with many other kinds of fish, could be profitably preserved in tins for export. There are in Galway about three hundred fishing boats, but around the bay as many more; at Boffin about fifty to sixty, at Achill thirty-five to forty, chiefly canoes (curraghs – R.C.). Inniskea, north and south, every family has a canoe. All along the peninsula of Erris Head, on both sides, Black Sod and Broadhaven Bay, perhaps two to three hundred canoes; round the Stags about one hundred more; but I cannot enumerate any creek without its own fleet of canoes.

Five to six hundred row boats and canoes could be employed without Galway Bay whose owners would be only too glad to have a ready market for their fish. This I will vouch for, having had many dealings with them, and having always found them willing to work when they were sure of selling their produce; but how galling to a crew of four men to find, when they had fished and taken forty large turbot in one shot of their lines, and then rowing to market sixteen miles through a heavy sea, to sell the whole lot for 25s., or sometimes less. *They often cut up turbot for bait for long lines.* The majority of these men require but little assistance in the way of gear or boats for fishing. I generally advance £1 to £3 for a canoe, sometimes more. I always supplied Indian corn to some remote villages in spring and summer, and took fish in exchange. *Each canoe on an average would represent one ton of dry ling, besides a quantity of other fish. I have often known three or four tons to one canoe in the season.* The fish can be contracted for early in the season at 5s. per dozen of thirteen, three feet long from the setting on of the tail to the back of the head, all under that length refused or doubled in quantity; summer price, 3s. to 4s. per dozen, according to locality. Thirty dozen ling will weigh one ton when dried and ready for market, at a cost of about £9 per ton.

Average price of ling for the last three years past, about twenty guineas per ton. It was last year twenty-six to twenty-seven in Dublin, and never during that time under £18, prime fish; cod-fish cost 2s. 6d. to 3s. per dozen, market price about £17 to £18 per ton, or barrelled for the London, Glasgow and other markets, or preserved in tins for export. Conger-eels, 1s. 6d. to 2s.; mackerel about 3s. per hundred of six score fish; hake from 1s. to 1s. 6d.; cod 2s. 6d. to 4s.; gurnet 2s. to 2s. 6d.

per hundred; glassen 1s. 6d. per hundred; and other small fish prices vary according to locality.

It is not possible within the limits of a letter to go fully into detail of the quantity of fish that may be purchased and caught on this coast, &c., were a proper and extensive system pursued, so that the men could have a certain market *at their own doors*, by employing agents to take it in. There is not a man on the coast that would not hail with rapture such an undertaking, and contribute largely to the success of it. This I will vouch, *for the men only want employ on sure grounds*. I pay on board the trawlers from 10s. to 12s. per week (no grub except coarse fish) to Claddagh men; they are thankful for that, sober and decent and good working-men, with sense enough to discard old prejudices (witness trawling), and eager for permanent employ; every man of good character can give security for money, gear or meal advanced to him.

There are something about four thousand barrels of herrings sold annually in Galway, which might be all supplied by one company at good profit, besides an enormous quantity of home-killed herrings and round fish, fresh and salt. Cadgers attend the market to buy, and come fifty to sixty miles, and were a constant supply kept their numbers would greatly increase.

It is not uncommon to take four or five hundred ling, besides eels, cod, &c., &c., in one shot of long lines – say three thousand hooks; *but with a large craft shooting double that quantity of hooks*, of course a proportionate increase might be looked for. Such a vessel could keep the sea, fish two or three boats, split and salt on board, and make up a full cargo in a short time: small open boats cannot venture out to the banks, therefore lose the best fish. These banks are now so accurately laid down in Captain Bedford's chart, that there is no difficulty in finding them out.

In my opinion it would be very desirable to get over a few Cornishmen for the herring and mackerel fishing in deep water; also a few Rush and Skerries men, for deep sea long lines, and a few Buckie boats and crews, as they are hardy fellows, and would come (without expense), an engagement being made with them to take all their fish. When the supply of fish would be so large a foreign market would be necessary – Spain or almost any of the Mediterranean ports – where any quantity can be sold before Lent. I cannot go into calculations at present – figures are easily put down – but my object is to state the truth unvarnished, and my firm conviction is, that a well-worked concern, conducted on an economical scale, and advantage taken of every opportunity, with first-rate trawlers' well-boats, and all necessary appliances, with capital to purchase at all times, would pay fully twenty-five to thirty per cent, and in very good seasons double it.

Oyster banks can be rented cheaply on the Clare side of the bay, six to nine miles off, any quantity of oysters can be had to lay down at about five shillings per thousand; in two years they will be in prime condition for market.

Should anything more be required of me I shall be most happy at any time to impart any information I may possess on the subject; or, if necessary, I would go to Dublin or London and answer any questions verbally that may be inquired. Apologising for not sending this last week, but I had a great deal to do on my return home.

I remain, my dear sir, yours very truly,<br>Thomas Wade.'

One further piece of testimony which Symonds obtained is worthy of notice by way of emphasising the stocks of fish then existing in Irish waters. It is from a report by a gentleman named Howard who, Symonds stated, had been fishing the North Sea and coast of Norway for the previous thirty years, supplying the London market with live fish and lobsters by means of well-boats. The report appeared in 1853 and the part quoted by Symonds is as follows: 'Having proceeded all round the southern coast from Cork to Breahaven, and from my own inspection, and from what I heard from persons of all classes, I have no hesitation in saying, both as regards quantity and quality, the banks off the coast and the Irish shores are richer in fish of all descriptions than those of any country I have ever seen. I spent a day and night at Kinsale

—the only place in the south of Ireland where the fishings are carried on to any extent. There are, I think, about forty hookers, the largest only thirty tons. Those being only half-decked could not with safety, I conceive, live in a heavy sea; and as not one of them has a well, the fish are killed as soon as captured and daily brought on shore; and I am further convinced that, from the inspection of all the fishing gear, that not half the quantity are taken that might be if the hookers were equipped in an efficient manner.

'I saw the fish on the morning of the 20th December when landing from the vessels; the cod, haddock and ling were very prime—the haddock, I am convinced, the finest in the world. I proceeded along the coast to Crookhaven, Bantry and Breahaven; at every place we found the fact corroborated as to the abundance of fish; but, except a few small boats in Glandore, Baltimore and Breahaven there were none to be heard of, as the fishing has nearly ceased from 1847, in consequence of famine, emigration and no market for the fish if taken.

'On returning from Breahaven to Bantry we came by boat and literally rowed across that fine bay through *a bank of herrings*; and I feel confident that, with nets such as those used in Scotland, the Isle of Man or on the Cornish coast, 40,000 barrels might have been taken that night; in fact the whole coast was swarming with them and would, if properly fished, rival Scotland in her annual take.'

With fish of the highest quality available in such quantities, often within a stone's throw of the shore, one may ask why the Irish lagged so far behind the English and Scottish fishermen in what they brought to market. The answer is undoubtedly in that one word 'market'—the almost total absence of which put a blight on the whole industry. Symonds puts the position very clearly: 'Those who have formed their estimate of a fisherman's life on the favoured shores of England and whose ideas are associated with fine, well-found boats arriving on some strand or quay whereon hundreds of buyers are ever ready to outbid each other for any fish that may be taken, can form no conception of the difficulties that fishermen on the west coast of Ireland have to contend with. Added to crazy boats, at best ill-adapted to the purpose, and imperfect gear, he is generally at such a distance from market that he becomes easy prey to the jolters, that is, cadgers or buyers of fish, and small curers who purchase at their own price; but when great quantity of fish is taken, having no capital to purchase it, that which is a harvest elsewhere is loss there. Thus, deprived of his dearly-earned profit, he is prevented from repairing his tackle and compelled to seek that sustenance from the land denied him in his legitimate calling. A division of labour ensues which is attended by prejudicial results to both; he is thus doomed to drag on the same miserable existence throughout the year without chance of amendment. Is it a matter of surprise, then, that thus deprived of the fruits of his labour, beggared even of hope, looking on all with whom he deals with suspicion and distrust, that he should become apathetic and improvident? No, the very principle of energy is destroyed. How, then, can he, poor, ignorant and trodden upon be otherwise? I have heard it often stated that they have refused to fish when, with the slightest exertion, they might have taken vast quantities. However, they have generally reason on their side, for of what avail would be the fish to them when caught if they had no market to sell it at or salt to cure it with?'

Some six or seven years before Symonds made his proposals, Wallop Brabazon had become interested in establishing a company to work the west of Ireland fishing grounds. Like the others, he, too, wrote a book, published in 1848, called *The Deep Sea and Coast Fisheries of Ireland*, in which reference is made to the skill of the local longshoremen as well as to their poverty. Brabazon writes: 'A company starting on the supposition that they were going to the west shores of Ireland to teach an ignorant set of men an improved mode of fishing by hiring English fishermen for that purpose, and thereby increase the take of fish, would fall into a very great error as no men can understand the hook fishing better than the west coast fishermen, and they could supply themselves with excellent baits unknown to strangers... I feel certain that if the fishing boats were well found in sails, rigging and plenty of fishing gear, it would pay the fishermen well (to work for the company)... I do not think that the crews of every tenth boat in Clew Bay have fishing gear but I have no doubt that if they were supplied with it by a company at a moderate price they would bring immense quantities of fish to their stores during the season.' The author then reveals that in the year ending April 1844, Ireland actually imported 127,770 barrels of herrings and 17,683cwt of cod, ling and hake, the bill for which came to £143,637, 'for food', as he says, 'with which its coasts abound'.

The unsatisfactory state of Irish fishing during the early years of last century was due almost entirely to inadequate markets leading in turn to the continued use of ill-adapted boats and unsuitable or insufficient gear. There was one other cause of which Symonds writes as follows: 'Were the fishermen united they could not only fish to greater advantage but bid defiance to all middlemen and salesmen who now prey on them at pleasure. The railways have in some measure relieved them from these drawbacks by placing them in direct communication with the factor at the principal market, and thus saving them from that rapacious land shark, the fish buyer for the wholesale market, who stands on the shore with jaws ever distended to swallow up the chief profit of the catch. Yet even this advantage is to some extent neutralized in Ireland by the constitution of the so-called "public" market which, unlike most others, is private property and therefore subject to influences that could never arise in a *bona fide* public one.' That will have a familiar ring for many longshoremen who have seen their catches retailing at three and four times the price they got for them.

Apart from all these impediments a general feeling of apathy and hopelessness grew up following the famine years of 1846-8 and reports tell of the desire to emigrate being so strong in many districts that even if constant employment were available few would choose to remain if given the means of leaving the country. About this time great numbers did 'go west' becoming the progenitors of future American presidents and policemen but it was many years before those left behind were able to put their fishing industry into a healthy state. Yet despite all their problems and shortcomings, the Irish developed three particular kinds of craft which are worthy of attention because most of their fishing was done in them. They were the curragh, often referred to as a canoe, the hooker and the wherry.

The first consisted of skins or canvas stretched over a light wooden framework, after the manner of a coracle, perhaps the earliest kind of boat man ever ventured afloat in. The Fisheries Officer at Queenstown, Lt W. H. Church, RN, wrote in an official report dated 26 November 1848, about the way they were worked. "The fishermen along the iron-bound coast from Loop Head to

A distinctive Irish craft: the curragh, made of skin or canvas, stretched on a wooden frame

Galway and about the mouth of the Shannon use a canoe, a framework of ash covered with canvas. These things are kept in the cliffs and launched, hauled up and shouldered with facility in places where no boat of wood could be used at all. They are about 24ft long, about 2½ft wide and 1½ft, or a little more, deep, and highly dangerous for unpractised people to get into at all, but in the hands of the natives do wonderful work and the said natives will go to sea in them in weather that any other people would not attempt in an open boat. A great number of them are now in the employ of the Dublin Fishing Company at Dingle and they bring in more fish in proportion to outlay and, I believe, than any other species of vessel.

'The men are obliged to sit low down in them and maintain the
sitting position which, for a whole night, is no joke and perhaps
none but the hardy Celt, subject to starvation, privation and hardship without feeling it, could endure the same. They go to sea in
them with nothing beyond their fishing gear save an iron pot for a
fireplace and turf to burn therein; their food, the first fish they
can catch, and if none is caught, they do with an empty belly.

'They commonly carry four men who pull two small sculls
each without any blade. The oars, having wooden lugs or ears
are shipped permanently down on the gunwale. These canoes can
compete in speed with our fastest gigs provided the water be
smooth and no strong headwind.'

Curraghs were used exclusively for line fishing and landed
immense quantities of cod, ling, haddock and hake. They were
cheap to build and in Church's time cost no more than a pound
or two. By the 1870s the price was around £5. Canvas eventually
superseded skins as a covering being thickly tarred and attached
in 2ft wide strips from gunwale to gunwale. In later times a small
sail was carried and set whenever there was a stern breeze.

Second, the hooker was a maid of all work, being used not only
for fishing but to carry passengers, collect seaweed and to serve
as a small coaster, taking freights like turf and manure. Many of
them, in fact, fished for only one month of the year, yet they were
highly rated, especially those from Dingle, as 'a poor man's fishing
boat'. With their sharp rising floor and long keel they were best
adapted to a deep-water coast where they could be kept afloat
They were smack rigged and often had their stay so taut that the
mast was buckled over the bows. The mainsail was loosely laced
to mast and gaff and besides a stay foresail some had a bowsprit
for setting a small jib. In the illustration I have included of
Galway and Kinsale hookers, taken from Holdsworth's *Deep-Sea
Fishing and Fishing Boats*, the nearer one is shown hoisting her
jib while on the other the pronounced buckling of the mast may
be observed.

The specifications to which many old-time craft were built have
disappeared, or never existed, because boat builders and ship
wrights seldom thought of putting them on paper. As I wrote in

The Irish hooker, used for cargo carrying as well as fishing

*Black-Sailed Traders* about the Norfolk wherry: 'You will find no plans, no drawings... With unerring instinct they (the wherry builders) knew what was right and what was wrong, and this instinct was a better guide to them than paper and pencil. An old shipwright once summed it up in a sentence—"If it's right it looks right, if it ain't it looks ugly".' That held true all round our coasts.

However, a complete specification of the Irish hooker has survived in the shape of an official document laying down the standard required for boats to become eligible for the grants available to help fishermen about the 1850s. I give it below without any alteration to the sometimes rather quaint spelling.

SPECIFICATION FOR HOOKERS, OF TEN TONS
OR THEREABOUTS.
The flooring Timbers to be at least 3½ inches.
The Foot-Hooks not less than 3¼ inches.
Top Timbers 3 inches, all dressed, to be of Oak; all the Timbers to be
not more than 13 inches asunder.

The Keel to be 21½ feet long, 12 inches deep, and 4 inches thick; to be composed of either White Oak, or Black Birch.

The Boat to be 6 feet deep, and to plum 9 feet in the beam.

The Plank to be of the best Quebec Red Pine, 1⅛ inches thickness, plained; not more than one but in each streak.

The Stern-Post to be of White Oak, same scantling as Keel.

The beams to be of White Oak, the main beam 4 inches thick, and 10 inches wide at least, the after beam 3½ inches thick, by 10 inches wide.

The keelson to be of White Oak, to cover 6 timbers, and to square not less than 7½ inches.

4 Knees to the main beam, 3½ inches thickness at the least.

2 Knees to the after beam, 3½ inches thick.

The rudder to be of White Oak, 4½ inches thick at the head, and 2 inches at the bottom.

A Counter stern, same scantling and stuff as plank, and a top moulding of Black Birch, all round, with quarter pieces of oak.

2 Transom knees of oak, 3½ inches thick.

The bow Gunwales to be of White Oak, 3½ inches square, and a fore-stool of 4 inches square, with 2 knees.

The breast hook, oak, 4½ inches thick.

The deadwoods, channels, and transoms, to be of White Oak.

The Ceiling to be same thickness, and materials as the plank.

The forecastle deck to be 1½ inches, and the after sheet to be 1 inch.

The ballast boards to be 1 inch thick, and platform under the fore-sheet, ¾ inches, and a seat across the stern, with all necessary cleets.

The Carlines to be of Red Pine, 4 inches, by 3½ inches.

The boat, to be trenailed, the iron work to be used same as pattern, to be seen at the depot, mast and bowsprit irons to be fitted to the spars.

1 Anchor of 56lbs. and 1 Anchor of 40lbs.

The best Norway spars to be used, of proper proportions:- Mast, 32 feet, - bowsprit, 14 feet, clear of cap; gaff, 14 feet; boom, 27 feet; and 2 sweeps, 18 feet each.

Hawser, of 3 inches, 50 fathoms, and 1 of 3½ inches, 50 fathoms.

Shrouds to be 3 inch rope, the stay of 4 inch. 4 strand, and an eye turned in the head, and the running rigging in the same proportion; all to be of the best first lay Cordage, and to be provided with New Blocks, of good quality.

### SAILS.

The mainsail, and foresail to be of No. 3, canvas, and the jib of No. 5, to be fitted with all thimbles, hooks, and other necessaries, and to be cut in proportion to the spars; the entire boat to be thoroughly caulked, and to get two coats of tar.

It is to be clearly understood, that the boat is to be completely finished, in all respects, fit for sea, in a workmanlike and unexceptionable manner, and subject to the approval of the inspector; and if any objection should be made to the whole, or any part, the point is to be decided by a reference to two master shipwrights, one to be chosen by each party, who, if they differ, may call in a third.

The boat to be measured by the Revenue Officers of the respective districts and to be paid for by the ton, according to their measurement.

These vessels were not called hookers because they engaged in hook and line fishing; the origin of the word dates back well into the sixteenth century when the Spaniards were much in evidence at places like Kinsale, Castlehaven, Berehaven, Valentia, Dingle, Smerwick and Galway. They used a small fore-and-aft rigged craft called an 'urca' which the Irish in time corrupted to 'hooker' or, as it is occasionally spelt, 'howker'.

The derivation of wherry, the last of the three types to be noticed, remains very much a mystery. When writing about the Norfolk variety in *Black-Sailed Traders*, quoted above, I put down all I had been able to discover: 'The word "wherry" was new to these parts (Norfolk and Suffolk) and must have been borrowed from the Thames, where rowing-boats of special build, and bearing this name, plied for hire in the manner of aquatic taxis. It came to be a generic term for many kinds of passenger-carrying craft, and we find wherries plying between Ipswich and Harwich, at Spithead and Gravesend, on the Tyne and even as far away as Ireland. But apart from the name they had little in common, being quite different in build and rig.

'Just why, and how, the word came to mean what it does remains a mystery. Some see it as a corruption of "ferry", others as a derivation from "wherret", to hurry, while another school of thought gives it a Scandinavian origin. This can hardly be so as there is no word in Icelandic, the tongue of the Vikings, Norwegian, Swedish, Danish, Dutch, Friesian or German from which it could possibly have come. And I feel sure it has no connection with a liquor, made in the West Country from crab apples, and called "wherry", from the Welsh meaning "bitter"!'

The Irish wherries were unique in being the only schooner-rigged fishing vessels in British waters. They varied in size from 30 to 50 tons, carried seven or eight men, and were much favoured on the east coast, particularly at Skerries. I discovered a note of their disposition in 1802 which shows that Ringsend had 5, Howth 7, Malahide 3, Rush 16, Skerries 36, Balbriggen 9 and Baldoyle 9. They were chiefly employed long-lining, not only in their own neighbourhood, but off the west and south coasts, landing large quantities of cod, ling, haddock and conger. Some

H

were decked, others only half-decked, and were sufficiently handy
to shoot and haul their lines using only the foresail. The illustration, from Wallop Brabazon's *Deep Sea and Coast Fisheries of*

The Irish wherry, only schooner-rigged fishing craft found in British waters

*Ireland,* shows a typical Skerries wherry of the 1840s with the
characteristic rake aft of the mainmast, rather similar to a Yorkshire coble. According to Holdsworth, only one or two were left
by the middle 1860s, and these appear to have forsaken fishing
for the coasting trade.

Besides great lines, long lines and hand lines, two other methods
of using the hook deserve mention: the feather lures so popular
nowadays with the Cornish mackerel fishermen, and the trot line
still widely worked in estuaries and on coasts which have long,
shelving beaches. Feathering for mackerel is much the same as
hand lining though the arrangement of hooks is quite different.
Instead of two or three there may be twenty or more, spaced along
the line several feet apart, on snoods only a few inches in length.
To the shank of each hook are whipped several brightly-coloured
feathers which, in Newlyn, so I am told, are imported specially
from China. A weight of from 8oz to 1lb takes the line down to
the required depth, indicated these days by an echo sounder. As
soon as fish are found the engine is throttled right back, the tiller

is lashed hard over, and the boat left to circle at slow speed while the crew get busy with the lines. The up-and-down motion applied attracts the mackerel to the feathers but in trying to seize them they take the hook instead. When several are felt to be fast the line is hauled in quickly hand over hand, then, with a jerk of the wrist, they are shaken off into the bottom of the boat. There is no pausing once a strike is made, down go the lines again, then up, with perhaps five or six fish on each. Provided the boat continues to move round over the shoal it takes only a few minutes to catch a hundred; but it can be quite exhausting while it lasts and unless you wear stout gloves your hands can get badly lacerated by the hooks during the shaking process. A sure sign that mackerel are about is when you see several boats circling over the same area; but shoals can be fickle and will suddenly move off for no apparent reason, when they have to be searched for again with the echo sounder. (See pages 103 and 104.)

The gaunt grandeur of the Cornish coast, the delightful coves to which the fishermen return, not to mention the fine mackerel you take back for breakfast, make this one of the pleasantest parts of England to go longshoring. There are fish in plenty, too, in the deeps about Land's End, like bream, ling and pollack; these can

Trot lining in the Thames estuary, about 1900

also be caught with feathers though strips of mackerel are generally put on the hooks as an added temptation.

For trot lines you need a very different stretch of coast, preferably where the beach is sandy, or sand mixed with mud, gently sloping so that at low tide a considerable expanse is left uncovered. The illustration shows a trot line in use at Leigh-on-Sea early this century and is reproduced from a sketch among the James Murie papers in the Central Library, Southend. It is the simplest way of all to go fishing as you require neither a boat nor elaborate tackle; and in rough weather, when you would probably not be able to get off in a boat, you can expect really good catches.

All you need is 30 or 40 yards of line and about 30 hooks attached to it with snoods a foot long. You will also need two good weights which can easily be made by filling medium-sized flower-pots with cement in which you bed a piece of galvanised or copper wire bent double to form an eye. A couple of herring, filleted and cut into small strips, will provide ample bait, or if you can dig your own lugworms so much the better. When baiting up I coil the line down on to a wooden tray which prevents tangles and allows it to be carried easily. At low water spring tides, that is when the sea is furthest out, go right to the water's edge and attach the line to one of the weights; then walk slowly backwards paying out line and hooks as you go and when you reach the end attach the other weight. If you set it almost parallel with the shore the wash of the incoming tide will carry each snood and hook clear of the line; set at right angles, hooks, snoods and line tend to become twisted up and you will catch fewer fish.

That is all you have to do. In about ten minutes the tide will have turned, your line will be covered and as the fish come in to feed they should hook themselves. You must now wait about twelve hours for the next low tide before you can inspect your line, but unless your luck is right out you should find half-a-dozen good-sized fish. Quite recently I set a line of 33 hooks at Hill Head on the Solent, the weather blustery with plenty of rain, and next morning collected 14 flounders, 2 whiting pouts, 4 bass and 3 mullet. Years ago, when old fishermen became too infirm to go boating, they managed to earn many a useful shilling working a few trot lines. Unfortunately, it is not a summer occupation; the shallow water then is alive with small crabs which will strip the hooks of bait in five minutes. Come winter and one or two hard frosts, however, and they all go to ground; that is when trot lines are worth the trouble of baiting and setting.

In the days when fishing was a parochial if not a family affair, all the bait needed was gathered by wives, sweethearts and children; as soon as the menfolk were away in their boats females and youngsters set off along the beach with baskets, forks and rakes to collect all they could lay their hands on that would serve as bait. While some fish may prefer one bait to another, in general, and when they are hungry, they will take anything. Soles, plaice and other flat fish, for instance, show a marked liking for lugworms, cod enjoy whelks with the shells removed, while conger eels are very partial to a chunk of fresh mackerel. But be the weather hard with feed scarce and there is little picking and choosing; a ravenous fish will gobble anything remotely appetising. Yarrell, for instance, in his *History of British Fishes*, tells us that a good bait for the grey mullet is the fatty entrails of fish and cabbage boiled in broth. I have never tried it but mean to one day.

Lugworms and ragworms have to be dug up and to get two or three hundred at a time can be quite a back-aching job. Cockles and mussels are more easily obtained with the aid of a rake, while slipper limpets, very popular on some coasts, can be dislodged from rocks with little effort. Whelks nowadays are taken in small pots which are themselves baited with any old bits of stale fish, but in the past small crabs would be slightly crushed and threaded on trot lines which, when hauled in, brought up hundreds of whelks still feeding on the crabs. So there was plenty of scope for the womenfolk as they prowled the beaches and it was a rare thing for them to return home without enough for the morrow's fishing.

But when improved roads and the building of railways put fish in demand all over the country, so great became the need for bait of all kinds that a distinct longshore industry grew up to supply it. Great numbers were employed procuring mussels and whelks in the Wash for the North Sea line fishermen, large quantities of sprats and whitebait from the Thames went for the same purpose, hence the name 'whitebait', while coast dwellers everywhere found it profitable to seek out the shell fish, then so abundant all round them, and send them to the nearest fishing port.

The drift fishermen and the Cornish pilchard seiners also reaped a useful harvest when their own markets were glutted.

Herring, mackerel and pilchards make excellent bait for all kinds of fish and the Plymouth men, for instance, would buy the latter from Falmouth and Mevagissey; Milford Haven often sent to Great Yarmouth for herring, sometimes even to Ireland for mackerel; in fact, whenever there was a surplus of these kinds of fish, the liners could usually be relied on to take them.

Hook and line fishing is still carried on in a few places but commercially it is just about dead. Once fish began to get scarce, as they did around this time last century, the hook became less and less effective; when trawlers arrived to sweep vast areas of the ocean bed the liners stayed ashore to avoid losing their gear, for these marine juggernauts not only scooped up the fish but the pots, tackle and lines of other fishermen which happened to be in their path. Eventually, the longshoremen themselves had to adopt the trawl and it is this method we shall be considering in the next chapter.

# CHAPTER SIX

# Trawls Oust the Long Liners

In comparison with other methods trawling has a comparatively brief history, being probably no more than two hundred years old. We cannot say precisely when or how it started though the men of Brixham in Devon and Barking on the Thames both lay claim to its development. The principle is such an elementary one, however, that in its crudest form it must have been made use of for thousands of years.

All it comprises is a triangular-shaped bag of netting drawn over the sea bed so that everything it collects, sea-weed, stones and rubbish of all kinds as well as fish accumulate in the apex, or cod-end as it is called. To do this the mouth of the net must not only be kept stretched open but the top has to be raised some distance from the ground. This is done by using a stout beam, usually of elm or ash, of the required length, to the ends of which are attached iron 'trawl-heads', that can slide over the bottom rather like a sledge. This is clearly shown in the illustration, which comes from Whymper's *Fisheries of the World*, depicting a North Sea smack towing her trawl on the Dogger Bank.

In time the rather cumbersome beam was discarded in favour of 'otter-boards', the invention of W. Hearder, a Plymouth man. The diagram, which originally appeared in F. G. Aflalo's *The Sea-Fishing Industry of England and Wales*, shows how these boards are forced outwards, rather like kites, by the pressure of the water as they are towed along, thus keeping the mouth of the net stretched open. To be effective, however, a fairly even speed had to be maintained, not always possible in a sailing craft, and the otter trawl was not, therefore, universally adopted until steam

127

took over from sail. Among the longshoremen, where sail survived much longer than it did on the open sea, the beam continued to be used and in places even now is still preferred to the otter trawl.

The first trawl to be used in the North Sea was towed not by a fishing vessel but by the Revenue cruiser *Greyhound*. She was one of the larger craft employed in this service and carried a crew of thirty-three. Some of them appear to have been Devon men used to trawling out of Brixham and when they were stationed on the east coast suggested to her commander that they should get a trawl and provide themselves with some fresh fish. This was in the late 1820s and although the commander agreed to the men's request not many fish were caught. Next came a William Soad from Ramsgate who worked close inshore off the Lincolnshire and Yorkshire coasts and made quite a good living. Three further trawlers then appeared on the scene working out of Grimsby but had no success until they moved on to Scarborough. Then came a smack-owner called Reding from Barking who did well with two

The beam trawl at work

of his vessels and more from the Thames soon followed his example. By the 1850s Grimsby was firmly established as a trawling port and its subsequent development was largely due to the extensive docks constructed by the Manchester, Sheffield & Lincolnshire Railway Company.

At first, when comparatively small vessels towed moderate-sized trawls, little exception was taken to this new mode of fishing; inevitably, however, bigger and bigger craft were built to work ever larger trawls, their numbers increased, and in their search for the most profitable fish, such as soles, they started operating close to the coast. This invasion of the longshoremen's traditional grounds caused considerable friction and a lot of ill feeling; not so much because the trawlers were taking the longshoremen's fish, though this was a charge levelled at them, but because the heavy beam often from 40–50ft in length, dragging over the seabed on its iron runners, tore away and destroyed the lines of the hook fishermen. These were nearly always shot athwart, that is, at right angles to the tide; so it was almost impossible for both to be fishing in the same area without serious risk of damage being done to the lines.

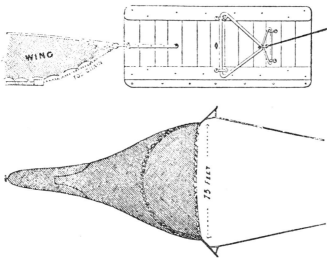

Diagram showing the operation of an otter trawl. In time, with the introduction of power-driven craft, it largely superseded the beam trawl

Drift-netters also suffered. As with lines, drift-nets are shot athwart the tide and with a fleet of them out, perhaps a mile long, a drifter was powerless to take any avoiding action should a trawler bear down on her. The situation was worst in Cornwall where trawlers fishing the Wolf Bank between the Lizard and Land's End were constantly fouling the mackerel nets of the Penzance men. Few of the trawlers were local boats, most of them hailing from places like Dartmouth and Plymouth. Many accounts were given to the two Inspectors of Fisheries, Frank Buckland and Spencer Walpole, sitting at Penzance in 1878.

A certain John Madden set the scene; he had been fishing from Mousehole for thirty-two years. When he began there were seven or eight trawlers there working from the end of February to the end of April. They did not interfere with the 'drivers' (drifters) because they used to heave up in the day and come in. They ran to Plymouth with their fish. Since the railway had opened the trawlers had increased every year. There were above a hundred there that year. They trawled south of the Wolf Rock from two to eight leagues from the land. They trawled night and day on ground that was the best for mackerel fishing. Drifting for mackerel went on only at night, they shot their nets at sundown and hauled them before sunrise. He was accustomed to the Irish fishery where the trawlers hove up at sundown and went in and believed if the same thing were done in Cornwall there would be no complaints.

He told of the experience he had on the night of 21–22 March last when drift fishing in the Dart south-east of the Wolf Rock. It was dark but starlight with very little wind. A trawler, 331 P.H., fouled his nets. She was 600 fathoms off. He hauled on his nets and warped up to the trawler when he was able to see her number. The trawler cut his nets away and those outside the trawler were cut adrift. He found some of them afterwards but lost six nets completely, valued from £12 to £15. Also lost his night's fishing. That same night was fouled by three other boats, 3 P.H., 29 D.H. and 122 P.H. Believed that trawlers should have been made to heave up their gear at night, as in Ireland, where a government cruiser compelled them to do so.

Many other witnesses were called and gave similar evidence, from which it is quite clear that the majority of trawlermen were selfish and unscrupulous, chose the ground that suited them best, even when drift-nets had been shot, knowing that they themselves would suffer no loss or damage. And if they saw drifters preparing to shoot on favourable trawling ground they did their best, in many cases, to scare them away. Richard Pollard, of Newlyn, complained about trawlers deliberately sailing short tacks around them to drive them off, but in the dark it was usually impossible to see their numbers. Others spoke in much the same vein.

Despite these enquiries, petitions and requests for a cruiser to be stationed in the area, the driftermen obtained no real satisfaction. This was very probably due to the fact that whereas the mackerel boats were individually owned by the longshoremen, the trawlers were being sent to sea by companies in which large sums of money were invested; when that is the case it is the small man who invariably goes to the wall. Authority may also have held its hand because of the substantial landings from trawlers, urgently needed to meet the ever-growing demand, and because the new method was seen as the only way of continuing to satisfy that demand in the years to come. If such arguments were used they have been amply justified as the bulk of all the fish sent to market nowadays is caught by trawl net in one form or another.

The Sea Fisheries Act of 1868 did, however, make some effort to regulate the conduct of drifters and trawlers. Article XV, for instance, laid down that 'Trawl boats shall not commence fishing at a less distance than three miles from any boat fishing with drift nets. If trawl boats have already shot their nets, they must not come nearer to boats fishing with drift nets than the distance above mentioned.' This looked well on paper but took no account of the practical difficulties inseparable from sail. Assuming a trawler observed the three mile limitation, shooting her gear to windward, in a good breeze she could not help driving down on to the drift nets as her speed over the ground would exceed that of the drifter being carried by the tide alone. Again, if in very light airs she shot to leeward, the drifter would have the greater speed and eventually foul her. With fleets of boats working in a restricted area there was bound to be trouble of one sort or another but the conduct of the trawlers generally left much to be desired; they were less vulnerable than the drifters and knew they held the whip hand when it came to a showdown.

Even so, the Devon and Cornish trawlermen never behaved as their Belgian counterparts did on the east coast where the herring nets of the Great Yarmouth and Lowestoft boats were regularly ripped apart by a device called a 'devil'. It was shaped rather like a grapnel with the arms ground to form sharp cutting edges and was thrown over the stern of the trawler on a ten fathom length of rope or chain so that a way could be hacked through the drift-nets. The object was not only to clear a passage for the trawler; in the darkness it was easy enough for her to haul in the separated part of the herring net and carry it off, along with the catch, to Ostend where it could be sold for the benefit, of course, of the skipper and his crew.

Belgian boats were the scourge of east coast driftermen during the 1870s and 80s and countless examples could be given of the losses they sustained in nets and fish. In 1875 the *Isabel* had 25 nets cut away with warps and buffs; the *Hosanna* lost 65 nets; the year before the *Sole Bay*, out of Southwold, lost 120 nets, as did the *Beatrice*, also from Southwold. At an enquiry held at Lowes-toft to look into the mounting number of complaints evidence was taken from one Daniel Durrant who said: 'I am master of the fishing lugger *Morning Light*, belonging to Messrs. Robert and Frederick Capps. Her tonnage is 28. On the night of 17 October I was at sea with my drift-nets down and during the night my nets were cut in two by a foreign trawler, which I knew by his rig, and which had no lights up, but we had ours as usual. We could not put our small boat out because there was too much wind and we were, therefore, unable to find her name or number. The damage was £50 besides loss of fishing; my warps were cut also. We lost seventeen bowls as well, which are small casks bound with iron, costing 3s. 6d. each, and other damage was com-mitted besides. On 27 October we were again at sea fishing for herrings in the same vessel and we put our nets down about 6 p.m. Soon after 7 o'clock a trawler, with 0.144 on her bows, but without any name, crossed our nets and rent them a good deal, his trawl being down. We lost 12 of the nets altogether of the value of £15. She was half a mile from us when she came through our nets. He had his green lights up and put his gear down about a quarter of an hour before he came into our nets. It was a clear night. As soon as he struck us we put our boat out and five hands went aboard of the trawler, and then we saw her letters and number. My crew helped the trawler's crew to get clear of our nets and were so engaged five hours. The crew told my crew that their skipper had been drunk ever since they had been out, and he was drunk then, and one of the crew told mine to report him at the Custom House. He further said that the crew had warned him that there was a herring boat, with her nets down, and he replied that he should put his trawl over, and he did. We recovered our nets but lost our fishing two nights through this and this affects ourselves as well as the owners.'

With these few instances taken at random we can have some sympathy for the sentiments, if not the spelling, of the fisherman who wrote to a local paper as follows:

To the Editor.
Sir,

I am master of a Lowestoft fishing boat, and I and my mates would like to know what orders the gunboat *Rose* have got; if she was near a french boat wen it was cutting a Lowestoft boat's nets, what could she do to them? Could she take the crew aboard of her and bring them hear, or could they give'm a jolly good trounsing, or would england declare war, or what I should like to know.

Your servant,

James ——.

While these matters were going forward off the coasts of Norfolk and Suffolk, something of very much greater significance was taking place off those of Yorkshire, Durham and Northumberland. Steam vessels, in the shape of paddle tugs, were trying their hand at trawling and coming back with some useful catches.

Their normal job was towing collier brigs and other sailing ships into and out of harbour but as it fell slowly into decline with the advent of screw steamers they were forced to look around for other employment. In flat calms they had often given a friendly pluck to trawlers with their gear down, thus enabling them to get a few fish where otherwise they would have got nothing, and so, no doubt, they had the idea of taking a trawl to sea themselves while waiting for a 'job' to turn up. Long before this, and to while away the time, one or two tugs would shoot lines and usually returned to port with a few baskets of fish even if they had no ship in tow.

1877 seems to have been the year when these paddlers fitted themselves out with the necessary gear, shipped a couple of extra hands as fishermen, and went out to trawl instead of to tow. Not surprisingly, it was from Newcastle that most of them went, the 'coaly Tyne' having hitherto been the port of departure for thousands of brigs, brigantines, snows, schooners and ketches engaged in satisfying the ceaseless demand of London for fuel. The tugs were there to give them an offing when bound away deep-laden or to help them in when returning light. But with steam coming more and more into the picture and threatening to take over completely from the sailing coasters, the tugs were forced to cast around for alternative employment. For several years fishing provided it but, as we shall see, such is progress that eventually they were hoist with their own petard.

At first they did little more than 'go longshoring' seldom being out for more than twenty-four hours at a time, often long enough however, during December, to catch 20 or 30 baskets of haddock as well as soles, plaice and cod. The trawler-tug *Patriot* may be cited as a fair example of how these vessels were worked, she being one of some thirty-two which towards the end of 1877 were fishing from the Tyne. They varied between 10 and 20 tons register, carried two hands as fishermen in addition to their normal complement of four, and were valued at around £2,000 each. The *Patriot* was owned by John Robert Lawson and her gross weekly earnings used to range between £12 and £56. Expenses for coal oil and tallow amounted to £5 a week, which was subtracted from the earnings, the remainder being halved between the owner and the crew. The crew's half was divided into six shares of which three men each took one share; the captain and first fisherman each had one share and a quarter, the lad, or sixth hand, a half share. Taking an average between the weekly earnings of £12 and £56 we have £34, which works out at £3 for the captain and first fisherman, £2 8s for the three hands, and £1 4s for the lad. The owner received £14 10s, or £554 per annum, out of which he had to meet interest on capital and wear and tear. Altogether a pretty satisfactory return bearing in mind that even when she was fishing an eye would be kept lifted for any vessel requiring a tow into harbour when extra money could be earned.

Sunderland tugs were equally to the fore, a very successful one being the *Cambria*. One of her extra hands shipped as fisherman was Thomas Palmer and he has recorded how they went trawling from the Coquet to Hartlepool and up to twenty miles from the coast, making very substantial catches of plaice, soles, cod, haddock, whiting, turbot, ling, skate, cat fish and monks. At this time there were sixteen hook boats working out of Sunderland, each carrying three men, besides hundreds more going off from adjacent beaches, and complaints soon began coming in of how their lines were being destroyed by the trawl nets dragging over them, how their catches were decreasing and how the spawning ground of many varieties of fish they relied on for a livelihood were being ploughed up and threatening them with ruin.

There appears to have been ample justification for these allegations. The following examples are taken from evidence given before the Inspectors of Fisheries in 1878, by men actively engaged in longshore fishing, which show how impossible it was to carry on line and trawl fishing on the same grounds at the same time.

Joseph Jefferson, of Alnmouth, said: He has been a fisherman for nearly 60 years at Alnmouth. Has never known such a bad year for haddock, cod, &c. as the past spring. Attributes the failure to the Tyne trawlers which come about the 1 March. They never came before this year. They work on the Coquet Smooth, between Warkworth and Boulmer, from 5 miles to 20 miles out. They sometimes come into 3 fathoms of water within a quarter of a mile from the shore. The trawl is down six or seven hours. The only time he was alongside the steam trawlers they were catching soles and flat fish. Thinks that the trawlers disturb the line fish and drive them away. The trawlers interfere with his lines. They have taken away his lines once and this has also happened to other boats. His lines were worth £3. Thinks that it was wilfully done. The lines were shot at 4 o'clock on the Monday morning and after they were half hauled, at 5 o'clock, seven or eight trawlers came down and trawled north into the Coquet Smooth. Warned one of them but she paid no attention. Could see her number, she was the *Flying Cloud*, of Shields. When the trawler was fast to his lines he refused to haul up his trawl. Afterwards recovered part of his lines and so abstained from taking proceedings. Thinks that no trawlers should be allowed in less than 40 fathoms water.

Robert Taylor, of Alnmouth, said: He has been fishing above 35 years. There are six winter fishing boats at Alnmouth and five in the summer. There have been thirteen. In the winter they are line fishing. The Alnmouth men fish from Craster on the north to Creswell on the south, and from 5 to 20 miles out, but when the weather is bad they are not half a mile out. The line fish have fallen off greatly. Used to be able to get more on one line than he gets on six now. The trawlers began last spring in the first week of March. Thinks the trawlers drove the fish away. There have been 27 to 30 trawlers among the line fishermen. They have been driven away by the trawlers because they are afraid of the trawlers taking their lines. Has had his lines broken. Thinks no trawler should be allowed within a certain distance from an open boat fishing with lines or otherwise.

George Stevenson, of Boulmer, said: There are 10 line boats at Boulmer, 14 in the herring season. There are more lines in the sea than there were when he was a lad. The price of the fish is better but they have fallen off greatly. They had not fallen off before last spring. They began to fall off after the trawlers came. There were 20 steam trawlers on the Coquet Smooth this spring. The Coquet Smooth is about 7 miles long by 2 miles broad. The trawlers have frightened away the fish.

Robert Kerr, of Cullercoats, said: He has lived 50 years at

(*above*) Cornish crabbers of the 1870s

*Page 137*

(*below*) Cromer crabbers of the 1970s

Carr Rock, Spittal

(*above*) Dragging for salmon at Spittal about 1912

*Page 138*

(*below*) Dragging for mackerel at Budleigh Salterton, June 1905

Cullercoats, is now a fish buyer. The line fish have much fallen off since he was a young man. There was one boat last week lost a whole fleet of lines which were taken away by a trawler and there have been hardly any line boats fishing since. The only boat that has fished lately has had all its lines taken away. The men have lost their great line gear and have now none to use. There are 43 boats in winter time. There are three men and a boy in each boat and perhaps three wives and twelve children dependent on each boat. There are, therefore, about 800 people in Cullercoats dependent on fishing. These people are all more or less dependent on the line fishery and the steam trawlers are doing a fearful mischief to the lines. A fleet of great lines is worth about £7. If there was a law making the trawlers give compensation it would be all that could be reasonably asked.

John Brown, of Newbiggin, said: He goes line fishing in the winter and fishes for herrings in the summer. Fishes in the winter between Coquet Island and Newbiggin Point, and from 2 to 12 miles at sea. Has counted 25 or 26 trawlers on the ground. There were no steam trawlers here before last October. There have been sailing trawlers here for 12 or 14 years at chance times in the spring, chiefly from Grimsby. They sometimes did harm. But the sailing trawlers can only trawl with the tide, the steam trawlers can trawl against it. This year lost one line and a buoy on 28 May. Was with his lines. Saw the trawler come on them. Hailed him but could not see his number as it was painted ahead on the paddle box. She was 200 yards off. On another occasion the *Fury* trawled over his lines. Warned him not to come but he trawled over the lines and took away those of five boats. Applied to the harbour master of North Shields and obtained the name of the owner of the tug. Thought that taking proceedings would be throwing good money after bad. In most cases where fishermen have been fouled by trawlers they have seen the boats coming. It is generally by day that these occurrences take place. The line fishermen have not fished at night since the trawlers came. The great lines used to be put out in February but they are now done away with by the trawlers.

A great deal more evidence could be quoted, of a similar kind,

J

showing how the longshoremen of the north-east coast were
gradually forced to stay ashore when it was no longer profitable
or even practicable, to shoot their great lines and long lines
Equally hard hit were the crab and lobster fishermen whose
shanks of pots were regularly cut adrift and lost, while the brat-
net men, who set anchored nets on the bottom to catch mainly
turbot, soon had to bring their gear in where it was stowed away
and left to rot.

But it was only a matter of a few years before these trawler–tugs
had cleaned out all the workable inshore grounds so that there
were virtually no fish either for them or the longshoremen to
catch. Yet while they had flourished, and the longshoremen de-
cayed, their owners had put by some nice little sums and were
more than willing to discard these ramshackle remnants of a
bygone age in favour of the custom-built steam trawler: a vessel
fully capable of leaving the coast and going deep sea, out to the
Dogger Bank if need be, where sailing trawlers, large and well
built, had for many years been showing healthy returns. So the
days of the paddle-wheel trawlers came to an end. They had
caused havoc in the longshoremen's traditional fishing grounds,
made destitute thousands of families whose bread and butter was
earned on the sea, and started a decline in beach fishing from
which it was never to recover. Admittedly it was the north-east
that suffered first but once the potentialities and profits of steam
came to be appreciated no fishing ground anywhere was safe from
its exploitation.

It was, perhaps, at this point in time, about 1880 or soon after,
when the conserving of our fish stocks might have been attempted
with a reasonable chance of success. Clear and effective legislation
internationally agreed and rigorously enforced, might have kept
the stocks round our island safe from the depredations to which
they were so soon subjected. Some foresight and good management could have ensured that the numbers of captured fish did
not exceed their capacity for reproduction, making due allowance
for the limited knowledge then possessed of fish habits, spawning
grounds and the time needed by different varieties to reach matur-
ity. Unfortunately, the social conscience and the climate of public

opinion was far removed from such a conception; it was a period of intense exploitation everywhere and the sea was no exception. At the International Fisheries Exhibition held in London in 1883, the Duke of Edinburgh proclaimed in a paper delivered there— 'With regard to the idea prevailing that the supply of fish is diminishing and that this is due to over fishing, it must be borne in mind that most species of fish prey on others and that the impartial depredations of man do not disturb the balance of nature on which depends the power of reproduction of each species.' On every hand, with few exceptions, the cry was the same, 'hands off the fishing, the seas are inexhaustible'. One of these exceptions was James G. Bertram, author of *The Harvest of the Sea*, who wrote as early as 1865—'Blunders perpetrated long ago in Encyclopaedias and other works, when the life and habits of all kinds of fish, from the want of investigation, were but little understood, have been handed down to the present day, so that even now we are carrying on some of our fisheries on alto- gether false assumptions, and in many cases evidently killing the goose for the sake of the golden egg; in other words, never dreaming that there will be a fishing tomorrow, which must be as important, or even more important, than the fishing of today, beyond which the fisher class as a rule never look.'

It may be over-generous to say that the implications of the tremendous catching power of the steam trawlers were not appre- ciated at the time; indeed, precious little thought was given to the matter at all as they returned from trip after trip with all the fish they could carry. In the general free-for-all the waters round our shores were savaged and exploited just as the great virgin kauri forests of New Zealand were hacked down and destroyed. Nature, over the centuries, had provided trees and fish in abundance, but man had not the wit to treasure and husband these priceless stocks; for him, a standing tree or a swimming fish meant one thing only, ready cash, so he axed and trawled till nothing was left. Fortunately, grass grew where once the trees had been, so that sheep might graze and a new wealth be produced; but in the deep of the sea where night and day the plundering goes on without respite, nature has no chance to heal her wounds.

With the passing of time the trawl net has been modified and developed into an ever more lethal instrument of capture; it need no longer be dragged over the seabed, though this is still done, but may be hauled along wherever the echo-sounder discovers fish to be, either near the surface, in mid-water, or close to the bottom. The fish have no sanctuary, little chance of escape, though what few remain must be hunted for with ever more ingenious scientific devices. The word fisherman is now something of a misnomer; he could better be described as a 'fish-mechanic', for without his electronic boxes it is extremely unlikely he would return to port with a couple of baskets of fish. So much reliance is now placed on this equipment that many will tell you they would feel completely 'blind' without it.

As more and more hook boats were driven off their rightful fishing grounds by the activities of the trawlers, the fleets of thousands of small craft that once sailed out from the beaches and harbours soon became just a memory. The majority of their crews turned their backs on the sea for ever and sought a new way of life in field or factory. Some, unable or unwilling to make the break, fashioned their own diminutive trawl nets and, adapting themselves to the new method, managed to earn a passable livelihood. The most successful were those who fitted a fine-meshed cod-end and went shrimping. The word 'cod' used in this context does not refer to the fish; it is of Anglo–Saxon origin and means a bag, or purse. Thus, the cod-end is that part of the net which eventually holds or contains all the fish which have entered at the mouth.

Many districts became famous for their shrimps, or prawns as they were sometimes called locally, and for years the supply of these small crustacea was barely able to keep pace with the demand. In the east end of London they were probably second only to jellied eels in popularity while no visit to the seaside was considered complete without a shrimp tea. Enormous quantities were sent up to Billingsgate every day from Leigh-on-Sea and Gravesend and business was equally brisk in places like Harwich, Southwold and Great Yarmouth.

Whatever evils may, in general, be attributed to the trawl net,

it cannot be denied that it alone created this demand for shrimps
by making possible their capture in large quantities. In Chapter 8
I shall have more to say about these shrimp fishers, but let us
move on now to consider some other appetising dishes which only
longshoremen provide for us.

# CHAPTER SEVEN

# Treats and Delicacies

Oysters, lobsters, crabs, scallops and salmon trout; how mouth-watering is the mere recitation of their names. And with prices what they are I make no apology for calling them treats because you need a very deep pocket to have them regularly on your table. For most of us they have become luxuries reserved for those special nights out when something a little different is called for to accompany an amiable bottle of Chablis or, perhaps, a Pouilly-Fuissé.

Even so, the menu will probably only include oysters and lobsters. Nowadays, crabs, scallops and salmon trout, or sea trout as they are often called, have become largely domestic dishes to be prepared by the housewife and eaten at home. All of them, however, have one thing in common, they are caught for us by longshoremen using traps and nets which are much the same now as they were two hundred years ago, and on grounds mostly inaccessible to big boats. Had this not been the case such delicacies would all long since have been swept up to appear no more on menu or fishmonger's slab.

As with most other kinds of seafood, however, stocks were seriously depleted in the past through indiscriminate fishing and this is one reason why oysters, for instance, are now comparatively scarce and expensive. Quite recently at West Mersea, in Essex, I saw them on sale at £2 a dozen within a stone's throw of where they are dredged, and could not help thinking of how they were once hawked round the London streets to the cry of 'Twelve pence a peck, oysters!' A peck, I might add, comprising two gallons dry measure.

144

James Murie believed that at one time they were plentiful everywhere in the Thames estuary but because of over-fishing the beds were gradually destroyed. He recalls what happened about the middle 1860s when fishing at Leigh-on-Sea struck a dull patch and fifteen boats began to search about for oyster beds in the area. 'They dredged along the Sheppey coast from Garrison Point outside of Cheney Rock buoys to the Cant edge. There they worked for about two months obtaining very large, middle-sized and small oysters. The average take for each boat was about three pecks a day which they sent by rail to Billingsgate. They were very fine old natives and sold at seven shillings per peck. Unfortunately, as has happened before elsewhere when a natural bed of oysters has been found, they were "scooped right up".'

Luggers oyster dredging

Oyster dredging may well be the oldest established of all our English marine industries for as long ago as AD 80 Julius Agricola was exporting considerable quantities of them to Rome which had been taken off Reculvers (Regulbium). These may well have been for laying down in the Lucrine Lake at Baiae for, as Pliny tells us, in the days of Lucius Crassus they were taken there to fatten from natural beds at Brindisi. The oyster was held in high esteem by the Romans and the great historian Sallust, who was, we are told, 'expunged from the list of senators in consequence of his shameless debaucheries', when speaking of this land of ours some fifty years before Christ said, 'The poor Britons—there is some good in them after all—they produce an oyster!' There can be little doubt that for at least three centuries Rome became the Billingsgate for the oyster dredgers of the Thames.

In the two thousand years which have passed since then oysters have continued to thrive in the Thames with those from Colchester, on the Essex side, and Whitstable, on the Kent side, taking precedence for quality and size. The fishery at Whitstable, however, came to an end some years ago which was not altogether surprising for in the late 1920s complaints were made that the people there 'Won't clean the ground of starfish, etc., and do the rest of the cultivation. Most of the time they are too idle to do more than just sit.' Ten years after, in 1936, I lived for a while not far from Whitstable and I got the impression then that the fishery was on its last legs. But there was still quite a fleet of smacks, called locally yawls, in the anchorage, though it was only rarely you saw them actually at work. They were originally clinker-built, with an overhanging counter, measuring from 10 to 25 tons burden, and were cutter rigged with boomed mainsail, topsail, foresail and jib. They were not strictly speaking yawls as they had no mizzen. Bawley boats, once a common sight on the Thames shrimping, were also used by the oystermen. They could be distinguished from the yawls by their straight-cut sterns and boomless mainsails.

To get properly fat oysters need the right kind of soil on which to lie and the water covering them must be neither too fresh nor too salt. At Whitstable this fresh water flowed over the beds from freshets draining the marshes between there and Faversham Creek. Wherever good oysters are found there, also, will be found the proper admixture of fresh and salt water.

They are brought up from the seabed with dredges, small,

triangular iron frameworks to which stout netting is attached, resembling somewhat diminutive trawls. Each smack, in the old days, worked a fleet of five or six dredges, two from the bows, two amidships and two from the stern, by which arrangement they were kept clear of each other as the vessel sailed or drifted with the tide. The towing warp of each dredge was coiled on deck with the end buoyed, being secured only by a short length of twine called a 'stop'. This was in case the dredge became fouled on some obstruction when the stop would immediately break under the strain, the warp would be carried over the side and the buoy would mark where it was so that it could be retrieved later. In the river Fal there is still a considerable fleet of sailing oyster boats but at Helford a very old and quite different method is used. Having dropped anchor and been carried away a suitable distance the vessel is then winched back hauling her dredges; by slightly altering the position where the anchor is dropped this manoeuvre can be repeated until any particular area has been thoroughly dredged or the day's quota obtained.

Many of the beds to which oysters were transplanted for fattening were often claimed to belong to some ecclesiastical or manorial estate; the Abbey of Faversham, for instance, enjoyed the right of fishing within the manor of Milton up to the dissolution when it passed to a company of 'Free Dredgers' governed by rules and by-laws agreed upon at the court-baron of the manor. Inert and placid as the oyster itself may be it has none the less been the cause of much rancour and ill feeling among coastal fishermen, nowhere more so than in the Thames between the men of Kent and Essex. Even in recent times it is alleged that east coast boats pay clandestine visits to Newtown in the Isle of Wight and dredge up stocks which the Hampshire men claim are rightfully theirs. Perhaps the biggest flare-up occurred in the eighteenth century at Hadleigh Ray, a creek near Leigh-on-Sea. In 1714 Sir Francis St John granted the fishing rights to one William Utton who began cultivating oysters with brood, so it is said, from Jersey, Falmouth and Ireland. He met with great success and in a few years had amassed a considerable fortune. This so excited the jealousy of the Whitstable men that with an armada of more than a hundred

An oyster dredger

smacks they crossed the estuary and sailed into the Ray with flags
flying and guns firing. They then set about dredging up William
Utton's oysters and succeeded in carrying off no less than 1,000
bushels. But they were to pay dearly for their spoils; when Utton
took them to law the case was heard at Brentwood and he left the
court having won his claim for £20,000 damages. In 1724 that
was a very large sum indeed, but it serves to show just how
important the oyster industry was in those days.

In the early part of last century there used to be quite a
reciprocal trade between the coast and country folk at Christmas
when enormous quantities of oysters were sent inland in exchange
for turkeys, geese, capons and other seasonable fare. The long-
distance stage coaches would be loaded right up with barrels on
the days just prior to Christmas, to the almost total exclusion of
passengers, and despite the assistance of two extra horses took

much longer than usual to reach their destinations. Oysters were not then a luxury food, as they are with us, but were enjoyed by all classes because they were plentiful and cheap. The poorest streets had their oyster rooms where the larger, less delicately flavoured specimens were to be obtained, while kerb-side vendors set up small tables opening each oyster as required. These dealers kept their supplies in tubs of water to which a handful or two of salt was added along with a little oatmeal; like this they could be preserved in good condition for several days, though this was seldom necessary with the great demand which then existed. The speed and dexterity displayed by the oyster sellers in opening their wares is often remarked upon by contemporary writers and in the illustration I have included we can see one of them in the

A street vendor of
oysters, about 1800

*"Fine Oysters!"*

act, so to speak, as she holds the oyster in her right hand and inserts the knife to cut the muscle near the hinge before prising the two shells apart. Some of the earliest representations of oyster fishermen and their smacks which I have come across appeared in the *Penny Magazine* for 24 June 1837; I have reproduced two of them together with an engraving from Whymper's *Fisheries of the World*, published fifty years later, which shows an interesting collection of the dredgerman's gear (pages 145, 148 and below).

The accepted way to eat oysters is from the shell, with a suggestion of vinegar and pepper, thinly-sliced brown bread and butter and champagne, though Londoners often prefer the more robust accompaniment of stout. Each one should be alive and consumed immediately after it is opened. Another, and very popular, method in Australia and New Zealand, though it may be considered sacrilegious by connoisseurs, is to remove the oyster from its shell, roll it lightly in flour, plunge in to moderately boiling fat to which several sprigs of parsley are added at the same time, and serve straight from the pan with slices of lemon.

The oyster dredger's gear

Oysters were once very widely distributed round our shores and besides the areas I have already mentioned considerable quantities were sent to market from Rochester, Queenborough, Maldon and the island of Jersey. During the 1830s and at the height of the season in the latter place, no less than 250 boats were kept at work and employment was provided for some 1,500 men and 1,000 women and children. Beds off the Welsh coasts supplied mainly the demand of local markets but in Scotland those from the Firth of Forth and Musselburgh Bay were appreciated everywhere for their large size and for their excellent flavour.

Lobsters and crabs were just as plentiful, and they needed to be, for as Adam White tells us in his introduction to *A Popular History of British Crustacea*, published in 1857, some of the largest shell-fish dealers in London at that time sold as many as 60,000 lobsters and 12,000 crabs annually. Just how many dealers there may have been is impossible to say but the yearly consumption, in the metropolis alone, must have been enormous.

Lobsters came to Billingsgate from as far away as the Orkneys and Shetlands, travelling alive in well-boats. Later they were sent by steamer, packed with seaweed in boxes, to Aberdeen and thence by rail to London. Yet despite this comparatively speedy transit they did not arrive in such good condition as when they were kept alive in the slower moving smacks. Flamborough, Harwich, the West Country, Ireland and the Channel Isles all contributed their quota and the number of welled vessels carrying lobsters probably exceeded those in the cod trade. Because lobsters, and crabs too for that matter, are only fit for human consumption when boiled alive, it was useless sending them to market dead. Hence the use of well-boats to bring them long distances, though this solved only part of the problem. On arrival in the Thames it might be found there was a glut at Billingsgate with prices ruling low in consequence, while in two or three days when the glut was cleared or when gales or calms had held up further deliveries, they might have doubled or trebled. As the boats needed to get away as quickly as possible on their return journeys recourse was had once more to the pond, or stew, which I have mentioned earlier as a storage place for flat fish, and to the floating box, or chest.

In 1876 Henry Barber, a Billingsgate dealer, had a large pond at Herne Bay which often contained as many as 2,000 lobsters. These would be sent up to London in batches when supplies were short and prices high. A Margate fishmonger always had a quantity available in chests with which to meet the requirements of his customers and the same kind of storage was made use of further up the coast at Queenborough. So far as the Thames was concerned the largest stocks would seem to have been held at Holehaven for James Murie records a conversation with an old man who said: 'I well remember when I was at school, in 1844, how we often went to look at the lobster boxes in Holehaven. They laid in long strings, perhaps fifty in a line, and were sufficiently buoyant to enable small boys to walk on them.'

Perhaps one of the biggest ponds of all was in Southampton Water, by the side of the river Hamble, which may well have owed its existence to the opening of the railway in 1840 which brought London, and its lucrative markets, within an hour or two's journey of the Hampshire coast. T. E. Symonds, from whose *Observations on the Fisheries of the West Coast of Ireland* I have already quoted, paid a visit there soon after it had been established by a Mr Scovell, 'in which,' he says, 'lobsters are kept alive in good condition for any length of time. The pond, or stew, is artificial, about 50 yards square by 10 to 12 feet deep, with shelving sides of brick or stone and cement, with concrete bottom, having a lock or weir at the entrance for the admission or exit of salt water, the Hamble being a fresh-water stream.

'The lobsters are fed on fish and fatten. On my last visit to the establishment, in August, 1854, there were 70,000 in prime condition although the summer had been very hot. All weak lobsters are kept in baskets and sold first. These lobsters are brought from the coasts of Brittany and Ireland, in sailing welled smacks of about 60 tons burden, which carry from 7,000 to 9,000 each. Mr. Scovell has several of these which are exclusively employed in this trade. He says the Irish fish are the finest but the voyage being longer is not so certain and attended with more risk, lobster carrying being subject to the following contingencies: thunder kills them in the well, also proximity to the discharge of ordnance. Mr. Scovell lost several thousand from the latter cause, one of his smacks having anchored at night near the saluting battery at Plymouth. Calms also destroy the lobsters in the well but onward or pitching motion in a seaway does not affect them. They keep alive one month in the well without food. The above causes have no affect on lobsters in the pond.'

The most ancient method of catching lobsters was with the hoop-net, a device still in use and which I have worked myself with considerable success. As the name suggests, it consists of an iron hoop, 18–24in in diameter, with a loose bag of netting attached to it, three bridles joined to a warp long enough to reach the surface when the net is on the bottom, with corks every 3ft or so and a buoy at the end. A double cord threaded through two pieces of leather is strung across the hoop and when these are brought together they hold the bait, usually old fish pieces, in the centre of the hoop. The object of the corks is to keep the warp and bridles clear of the net so that any lobsters which may be feeding on the bait at the moment of hauling will not be disturbed and back away out of the hoop. One of these nets is very easy to make and I contrived mine from some pieces of herring net and hoops salvaged from old casks. Commercially, this method has now fallen largely into disuse, the pot, or creel, being preferred almost everywhere. The Harwich men, however, continued hoop-netting for many years, mainly on the West Rocks, believing that the heavy barge and other coastal traffic would have damaged pots with their attendant warps and dan-buoys which had to be left sometimes for several days when it was too rough to haul them.

The smacks they used for lobstering were similar to the Whit-stable oyster bawleys already mentioned. They towed a heavy dinghy, 12–14ft long, in which fifteen hoop-nets were stowed aft. There was a crew of two only and when the smack was anchored on arrival at the grounds both got into the dinghy and began laying the hoops. One rowed while the other shot, great care being taken to ensure that each sank net downwards, otherwise nothing would be caught. With the last one gone they pulled back to the smack, brewed some tea, smoked a pipe or two and with a word about the look of the weather, went off in the dinghy again to begin hauling. This had to be done smartly, hand over hand, to prevent any of the catch escaping. And to stop them fighting once they were on board, which lobsters seem to do by instinct when removed from their natural element, sacks wetted in sea water were thrown over them. Later, when sailing back to harbour, the further precaution was taken of tying up their nippers. Around 1900 lobsters were sold on the quay at Harwich at about 10d per lb.

Lobsters and crabs are most abundant off rocky coasts which provide them with plenty of food and ample shelter. They will eat practically anything and one old writer has described their habits as follows: 'The bodies of all sorts of dead creatures are removed by the obscene appetite of these greedy crustacea; and there is no doubt that many an enormous crab, whose sapidity elicits praise at the epicure's table, has rioted on the decaying body of some unfortunate mariner.' He further likens them to wolves and hyenas which devour indiscriminately dead and living prey. The fisherman, therefore, has no particular problem over bait and although at Harwich they favoured slips, or small soles, for their hoop-nets, nowadays virtually anything is used in the pots. Very popular are the carcases of flat fish after they have been filleted; with few people eating fish on the bone these days they are in good supply and reasonably cheap. I was recently out crabbing in one of the Cromer boats and the bait being used was almost entirely carcases, obtained from Lowestoft, with a few salted grey gurnards.

The principle of the lobster pot, which will catch crabs equally well, is very similar to that of the old-fashioned, wire-meshed rat trap. It comprises a cage with a tapering entrance, sometimes two, making a funnel through which the fish has to pass to reach the bait, but once inside it cannot get out and stays trapped until the pot is hauled. The Sheringham, Cromer and Runton men use a very handy, rather flat, netted pot, with two entrances at the side and a door at the top fastened by cord ties, which is opened for

(*above*) Whelk boiling at Wells-next-the-Sea, 1972

*Page 155*

(*below*) Gathering mussels with the help of sleds at Leigh-on-Sea, about 1890

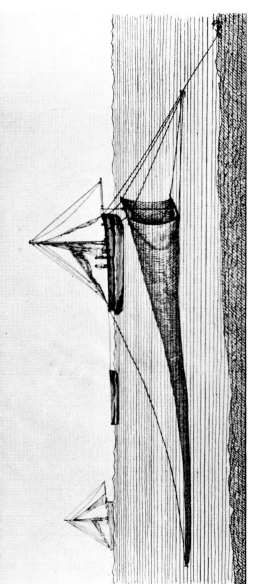

(*left*) Diagram showing how a stow net was rigged

(*left*) A kettle net. This ancient device remained in use on the lower reaches of the Thames till the late 1890s

baiting and removing the catch. They work 20 to 25 pots in a shank, anchored at both ends and marked by dan-buoys.

The willow pot of Cornwall is probably better known as it appears on innumerable picture postcards and is to be seen in most fishing villages there and in the neighbouring county of Devon. The locals swear by them as the best possible type of pot for the rough, rocky grounds on which they have to be used. They do, however, have certain disadvantages; after being in the water for any length of time they tend to become waterlogged and very heavy to handle, while it is not the easiest thing in the world to remove the catch once you have got the pot on board. This is clearly shown in the illustration of Cornish crabbers (page 137) where a kind of gaff is being employed to help lever out a particularly fine specimen. The Norfolk men who work five or six shanks to a boat, more than a hundred pots, have long contended that theirs are the most efficient and that the beehive-shaped willow pot would do little good at Cromer. They reckon them too big and heavy, too cumbersome and altogether unsuited to the quick emptying and baiting which they have to do. And with the entrance where it is, right at the top of the pot, they do not believe they have half the catching power.

Over many a pint and for quite a few years I used to argue the pros and cons with them till lately they agreed to undertake an experiment; I would send them two willow pots which they would work side by side with their own, then we could compare the results. Their contention was amply justified. With the Cornish pots they caught virtually nothing and although the season could not be counted a good one there were always one or two fish in their own. This should not be taken as a condemnation of the West Country pattern but rather as an indication that what is evolved to meet one set of conditions may be quite ineffectual where the conditions are different. The variety of boat types used round our coasts bears this out, though with the coming of the internal combustion engine the differences are not so pronounced as they used to be, and what is true of boats must apply equally to their gear.

The dictionary tells us that 'escallop' is 'a regular curving

K

indenture in the margin of anything' and that it is also 'the badge
of a pilgrim'. We know the word better as 'scallop' and think of it
more as a succulent bivalve which when opened rather resembles
a poached egg with its yellow centre and white surround. They
were cheap enough when I was a boy and made a handsome dish
for tea on crisp autumn evenings when the air had a nip to it and
one was glad of the crackling log fire. Like practically everything
else, however, they have now become scarce and expensive with
the result that probably few young housewives would have the
remotest idea how to cook them, even if they could afford them.

The old-time Thames fishermen used to leave the flesh in the
hollow shell, place it on a grid-iron over a clear fire and let it stew
in its own juice; then chopping it up, still in the shell, they mixed
in breadcrumbs, seasoned with salt and pepper and put back on
the fire for a few minutes to finish off. For those having neither
open fire nor grid-iron the scallop may be removed from its shell,
simmered gently in a saucepan for about fifteen minutes, chopped
into moderate-sized pieces and mixed with breadcrumbs, then,
after the addition of a little pepper and salt the whole returned to
the shell and set to brown for a few minutes under the grill.
Served immediately with a gentle squeeze of lemon is compares
very favourably with the fishermen's method.

Unlike crabs and lobsters, scallops are generally found on soft
or sandy bottoms and there seems little doubt that a hundred
years ago they were very widely distributed, perhaps more so than
oysters. Yet there was never the same specialised fishing for them
as for other kinds; they were sought for generally when things
were slack, especially the oystering, the same dredge being used
for scallops. During the 1850s three boats from Leigh-on-Sea
tried their luck scalloping 10 or 11 miles south of Worthing on
some beds they had discovered at a depth of 14 fathoms. They did
so well that by 1860 15 to 20 boats were working in the area. By
1877 40 craft from Dover, Folkestone, Rye and other Sussex
ports were actively engaged in the fishing, often joined from time
to time by a few smacks from Brightlingsea. Every week hundreds
of bags of scallops went sent to London while equally large quantities were sold along the coast. Right up to the end of the century

Folkestone and Dover fishermen found useful spring employment dredging near the Varne and Ridge shoals with sometimes as many as ten first class Brightlingsea smacks working the same grounds.

Scallops are often brought up in the trawls making a kind of bonus on the rest of the catch, along with the smaller variety, two or three times larger than a big cockle, but flatter, which are known as 'queens'. Many years ago I was in the Lowestoft motor trawler *Ala* fishing on Cromer Knoll when we took large quantities of these queens at every haul; they were thought of little account and went over the side with all the other rubbish, though nowadays they are in great demand. The rather unusual name queen is in fact a corruption of Quin. James Quin was a distinguished actor and older contemporary of David Garrick who lived from 1693 to 1766. Apart from his theatrical skills he had an equally great reputation as a gormandiser which Garrick delighted in alluding to in many of his verses. This 'Epigram on Mr. Quin' is a good example :

> Says epicure Quin, should the devil in hell
>  In fishing for men take delight,
> His hook bait with ven'son, I love it so well,
>  By G— I am sure I should bite.

In 1765 it would seem that Quin was in St Albans and there viewed the body of Humphry, Duke of Gloucester, who had been interred in the cathedral in 1447. The tomb was opened in 1703 when the body was discovered 'lying in pickle in a leaden coffin'. Getting to hear of this and being always anxious to have a dig at his great rival, Garrick penned the following two verses which he entitled, 'Quin's Soliloquy on Seeing Duke Humphry at St. Albans, 1765'. By then it is apparent the body had been wrapped up to make it rather more respectable, hence the opening lines—

> A plague on Egypt's arts, I say!
> Embalm the dead! On senseless clay
>  Rich wines and spices waste!

Like sturgeon, or like brawn, shall I
Bound in a precious pickle, lie,
    Which I can never taste?

Let me embalm this flesh of mine
With turtle fat and Bordeaux wine,
    And spoil th' Egyptian trade!
Than Humphry's duke more happy I –
Embalmed alive, old Quin shall die
    A mummy ready made!

Only a year after this was written Quin passed away to be buried himself in the Abbey at Bath, and soon his performances, on the stage and at the table, became no more than memories till at last they were entirely forgotten. Yet in 1840 the *Penny Cyclopaedia* could still say, referring to a particular way of cooking small scallops, 'they make a rich and sapid dish, as might be expected from the name of them when so prepared, "Quins".'

With his discerning tastes we may be sure that Quin's palate was often regaled with sea trout, that close cousin of the salmon, once taken in great numbers round our shores. Late spring and early summer was the season for them when they were swimming close in and the beachmen could ply their drag-nets. These are really small seines, 50 or 60yd in length, and require a minimum of three men and a boat to work them. They are roughly two fathoms in depth with corks to keep the backrope afloat and lead weights on the footrope to keep the net more or less vertical. At each end there is a pole sheathed at the bottom with more lead so that it stays upright to which bridles and a good length of warp are attached. One man remains ashore holding on to the end of the warp while the other two go off in the boat at right-angles to the beach, one rowing, the other paying the net over the stern. When about half of it is shot the boat begins to turn parallel with the shore, then gradually makes in back to the beach where one jumps overboard with the other end of the warp and the job of hauling in begins. The two warps are brought close together and when the net is reached the footrope is kept just ahead of the backrope which prevents too many fish escaping. As the area enclosed by the net gets less and less there is always great excitement especially when fish are seen leaping and splashing about. Should there be any mullet amongst them they will make desperate efforts to get free either by breaking the meshes of the net or jumping right out of the water and clearing the backrope. At last the bunt is dragged over the sand and with any luck there may be half-a-dozen trout besides a few dabs, soles, plaice and horse-mackerel.

Sometimes very surprising catches are made and the story is told at Southwold of some longshoremen years ago who went dragging for salmon trout one fine summer evening as daylight was fading and the moon was rising large and bright over the horizon. The net had been shot and they were slowly hauling in when there was a great commotion in the water and one reckoned he could see a white face with long hair trying to get over the backrope. They eased up on the hauling not knowing quite what to make of it when one said, 'Jimma, bor, dew yew mark what I say, thet there's a mermaid'.

They sucked at their pipes a bit apprehensively as they went on hauling and all the time their strange capture was making desperate attempts to get free.

'Never heard o' th' likes o' mermaids bein' caught on this part o' th' coast afore,' remarked the oldest of the three, 'but 'tin't t' say they in't around.'

'Well, looks as though we've found one and no mistake,' put in the third member of the group, who wanted to know what his companions thought they ought to do with her once she was safe ashore. This was discussed at some length as an accompaniment to the hauling, the conclusion eventually being reached that she could be exhibited in the town, at a small charge, which might provide the price of quite a few beers.

By now the creature had been drawn almost on to the beach and in the moonlight the white of its face, shoulders and back, down which streamed long tresses of hair, could be clearly seen. They strode down into the water intent on making sure of it when, with a struggle and much splashing, it rose up, on two perfectly good legs, and said: 'What kind of a game do you call this, then? Can't a girl go for a swim at nights without being molested by a lot of ruffians? Just you wait and I'll have the police on you,' with which she ran up the beach and disappeared.

Once at home she no doubt saw the funny side of it; certainly she never called the police if, indeed, she ever intended to. But it is a curious thing that the first recorded capture of a mermaid in England occurred on this very same part of the Suffolk coast in 1187. Unlike the one in our story, however, legend says 'it had no speech and after some months of captivity escaped by plunging into the sea'.

I used to do a fair bit of salmon trout fishing a few miles down the coast from Southwold choosing for preference a fine, warm, still evening in June and July; in cold, windy weather it is usually a waste of time putting a net in the water. On one occasion, in perfect conditions and with two local fishermen giving me a hand, we had only one small trout to show after three shoots and more than two hours' work. During this time and with darkness coming on we had noticed one or two flashes of lightning away to the south with an angry-looking sky building up over Southwold. One of my companions, Wilfie Wigg, a fine fellow and the best all-round fisherman it has been my privilege to know, reckoned we were in for a drenching and might as well get a roof over our heads while we could. With livid bunches of cloud mounting higher and higher incessantly rent with great jabs of lightning, it was no sort of weather to be out on an exposed beach. But the tide was now ebbing which meant we could shoot and all the time be carried towards our landing, which should not take much longer than getting into the boat and rowing there. I put it to Wilf, he rather reluctantly agreed, and with thunder now rumbling at our backs, we made a final shoot. We let the net carry as if we were drifting, for the further we went the nearer we got to the landing, and when at last we hauled were astonished to find nine splendid trout the largest of which went to more than 14lb. We never made out whether it was the change of tide or the gathering storm we had to thank for such a take but we were content enough, despite the tempest now almost upon us, as we winched up the boat, stowed away the gear and carried our catch in boxes along the sea wall. Wilf had just remarked on our luck in getting off with a dry skin when there was a mighty crack of thunder overhead which seemed to punch a hole in the black, whirling, over-laden clouds, for next instant the rain fell in hissing sheets; we took to our heels as best we could and managed to get indoors with oilskins streaming. It was then just before midnight and as we brewed up tea and drank it generously laced with rum we looked out on the most dramatic electric storm any of us could remember. We later learned that it had travelled from the south coast, over London to East Anglia and finally out to sea, but it took a long time doing it for it was not till 5 o'clock in the morning that the rain eased up and my companions could get away to their beds.

You seldom see salmon trout in the fishmongers these days but they are still fished for in various places, though catches are generally disposed of locally. At Barnstaple, in Devon, Mudeford, in Hampshire and along the Norfolk and Suffolk coast you can sometimes buy one, at a price, if you happen to be about at the right time. They are delicious eaten hot or cold and are quite simple to cook. For a hot dish cut into substantial steaks after heading and gutting, wrap well round with grease-proof paper and simmer for about thirty minutes or until the flesh comes away easily from the bone. Serve immediately with well-seasoned parsley sauce. If required cold, wrap a sufficient quantity of the fish in grease-proof paper, place in cold water, bring to the boil and continue boiling for five minutes, then turn off the heat and allow to cool. To serve, remove from the water and unwrap, drain for a minute or two, garnish with parsley and provide a side dish of cucumber steeped in vinegar, cored and skinned tomatoes and some sprigs of watercress.

I have dealt in this chapter with several of the luxury dishes we are able to enjoy thanks largely to the longshoremen; but we are just as indebted to them for all manner of other varieties, so let us look next at how some of them are caught, with a passing glance at the way stocks were once jeopardised by wanton and senseless exploitation. Fortunately they survived so that today things like cockles, mussels, whelks, shrimps, sprats and winkles, to mention only a few, are still to be had. Shell-fish stalls are where you are most likely to find the first three, so what better than to take a stroll round the nearest market-place?

# CHAPTER EIGHT

# A Pretty Kettle of Fish

Amidst the monotonous uniformity of stalls you find in present-day markets, displaying for the most part drab collections of machine-made rejects and bedraggled imported vegetables, it is refreshing to come across one engaged in the ancient and honourable occupation of purveying shell-fish. Refreshing in every sense, especially on hot summer days, when first you become aware of an unmistakable sea tang which, as you approach, slowly merges with the cooling scent of vinegar, a condiment inseparable from the enjoyment of all molluscs.

With whetted appetite you join three or four others already standing at the small counter and find ranged before you a number of diminutive white sauces heaped with enticing pyramids of cockles, mussels and whelks. Large bowls of them stand just behind and from these the proprietor, wearing usually a spotless overall and a not so spotless cloth cap, is continually replenishing the saucers. You will probably be greeted with a civil 'Good morning', but it is most unlikely you will be asked what you want; but do not worry, the procedure is simplicity itself. Bringing a saucer of whatever you fancy conveniently in front of you, and perhaps helping yourself to a slice of bread-and-butter usually on a plate in the centre of the counter so that all may reach it, you then sprinkle on some vinegar and possibly a sifting or two of pepper and salt from the utensils provided. Next, using thumb, index and second fingers, you convey the fleshy morsels, a few at a time, to your mouth.

You will almost certainly wish to have more than one saucer for after trying, say, the cockles there are still the mussels and whelks to tempt you. But remember to make a pile of your empty saucers for when you come to pay for your repast the proprietor will count them and charge you accordingly. As they are only about one or two pence each your bill will be a modest one, and the chances are you will have been regaled with much local gossip by your fellow trenchermen, about how the haymaking fares, the squire's pheasants, Fanny Brown's ninth and that so-and-so husband of hers, the spate of turnip flies this year and how the 'Blue Boar' looked like carrying off the darts trophy. You can certainly eat more lavishly and more expensively in hotels and restaurants but you will seldom meet the enlivening companion-ship and conversation you find at a shell-fish stall.

In the days when great and long lines were the chief means of catching cod, haddock, ling and other deep-water fish, the demand for mussels and whelks to bait them with was tremendous. Many fishermen went so far as to ask that the sale of mussels for human consumption should be made illegal on the grounds that this reduced the supply and put up the price. But it was not the mussels taken for food which caused the shortages; farmers were the real culprits, carrying them off by the waggon load to use as manure. Thousands of tons were taken every year for this purpose and the only cost to the farmer was some three-halfpence a peck to the locals for gathering them. This went on all round the coast wherever they were plentiful and where the beds dried out at low water. About 1850 there were several acres of mussel beds near Roanhead, on the east side of the Duddon estuary, but by the 1870s they had disappeared, most of them having gone for manure. So acute was the shortage about this time that the fisher-men had to import mussels from as far afield as Ireland and the continent to keep going at all.

This led Frank Buckland, then one of the Inspectors of Fisher-ies, to consider possible alternatives; these are the nine suggestions he put forward—a pretty kettle of fish, indeed!

1. Duhamel in his *Traité Générale des Peches*, 1769, tells us that the French fishermen of Picardy and Flanders used to pick up many common frogs and use them for bait, sticking the hook

through their thighs. There is an abundance of frogs in England which might be utilized in this way.

2. Duhamel says that common earth worms are not bad bait. When first caught they are somewhat tender, but when kept in moss for a week they become very tough and will remain a long time on the hook.

3. The black slugs which are abundant in some parts of England might also be tried.

4. Mussels might be gathered in different parts of the country, salted and sent to the long-line fishery stations. The Newfoundland men say, according to Duhamel, that mussels preserved in brine are not refused by cod, especially if they are soaked previously so as to get the salt out of them.

5. The inhabitants of Iceland use bits of fresh meat and, above all, the hearts of some sea birds which the fish catch and eat for food. The fishermen say they catch more than 20 fish with a bird's heart for every one taken with other baits.

6. When at Teignmouth I saw the fishermen catch enormous quantities of the larger sand launce and I was told there was no use for them. Why should they not be used for bait in the North Sea?

7. The common garden snail might possibly be used as bait. There are plenty of them about and they can be got at all times of the year; even in the coldest weather they can be found in clusters under old woodwork and outhouses.

8. I am not sure that cod would not bite well at lumps of bacon cut into the size of whelks.

9. I have it on a French authority that when bait for cod is scarce a portion of sheep's intestines will serve the purpose.

A junk cut from a cod's throat is also a killing bait. The only one I can vouch for from this bizarre list is number 8. Fishing from the deck of a battleship moored in a west Scottish loch and using a hunk of bacon fat scrounged from the galley I made a single catch of one 3ft dog-fish. I gladly accepted an offer of sixpence for it from a messmate. To others, who may have the stomach to try them, I leave the remainder of Buckland's ideas.

Mussels suffered through being too readily accessible; in most cases exposed at low tide they could be raked up and loaded into carts by the ton. At Leigh-on-Sea where the ground was soft they often had to be taken by sled to a convenient channel or gutway and there transferred to boats which brought them ashore (see page 155). They rarely had to be fished although quantities were frequently brought up in the oyster dredges. Similarly, long liners from Scotland and the entire east coast swarmed into the Wash and collected all they could carry away for bait, taking full-grown and undersized ones indiscriminately. As elsewhere farmers, too, played their part in helping to exhaust the scalps by using them for manure.

By an Act of Parliament in 1870 the Wash mussels were given a measure of protection; a close season was ordered during June, July and August, while two inches was the smallest size permitted to be taken. At that time seventeen scalps were under the control of Lynn corporation one of which, known as the Lower Daisly, was half a mile long and 300yd wide. As a result of the Act it was possible to send to market during the 1873–4 season, 2,480 tons of mussels, and in the following year, 4,452 tons, a very significant increase. They sold then for about £1 a ton so the return was quite substantial. London, Sheffield, Birmingham, Leicester and many other places benefited from these extra supplies.

Whelks have always been less vulnerable than mussels to the above kinds of exploitation chiefly because they are found only in fairly deep water. They could not be carted off the beaches and sandbanks and in any case were not, I believe, very suitable for manure. They were sought only for food and as bait for the North Sea cod lines. Wells-next-the-Sea, on the north Norfolk coast, has long been an important centre for this particular fishery; it continues to prosper because there is no apparent falling off in the supply or demand for these rather tough but very nutritious gastropods. The shell-fish stall I frequently visit on Salisbury market has them regularly, an indication of how widely distributed is this humble fare. They are caught in baited pots which resemble miniature Cornish willow ones for catching lobsters, but differ in having an iron base and framework bound round with small rope and tarred. The entrance is at the top, the bottom of the funnel being provided with a short valance of netting to prevent the whelks after they have got in, from crawling out. Most kinds of fish will serve for bait though when I was last at Wells I saw a ton or more of salted herring stacked up for the coming season.

Like mussels, cockles and winkles are creatures of the fore-shore, the first preferring sandy conditions, the second rocks or stones. Gathering them was usually left to the womenfolk, children and old men as no special tools or gear were required, apart from a basket or bucket, and a rake if they were after cockles. Most of us at one time or another have probably passed an hour or two down at the seaside scratching the sand for cockles and wandering among the rocks and pools picking periwinkles, but the professional gatherers were often at work most of the day so that they could add a few extra pence to the family kitty.

Winkles, or pinpatches as they are called in Suffolk, abound practically everywhere and enormous quantities used to be sent to London where they found a ready sale to the east enders. So popular were they that it was quite common for them to be sent from as far away as the Orkneys and Shetlands though Billingsgate in the main got its supplies from around the Thames and the many other east coast estuaries. Blythburgh Water, near Southwold in Suffolk, was a favourite haunt for 'pinpatchers' in the early part of last century though most of their 'catches' went to local markets such as Halesworth, Beccles and Lowestoft.

Cockling once gave employment to many old longshoremen who were past going to sea but refused to give up 'the fishing'. At Leigh-on-Sea any old boat would do to take them down to the flats where they could rake away contentedly and return on the flood with enough in their baskets to buy several ounces of shag and a pint or two at the local. The rather more ambitious used to go over to Sheerness dockyard and lay out a pound or two on some discarded admiralty craft. With a cuddy built on, the addition of a weather-strake and quite often a short mast and sail, they served their turn up and down the gutways and along the flats.

Norfolk has some exceptionally good cockling grounds especially on the north coast where the Stiffkey 'blues' are almost as famous as Whitstable 'natives'. Their name derives from the blue-grey tint of the shell, resulting in all probability from the muddy sand in which they are found. They grow to a fine size and are better flavoured than any others I have tasted, being at their best when served straight from the boiling water and eaten hot. There is much to be said for opening them like oysters and eating them raw, a method favoured by several kinds of sea birds. Some of the larger gulls will take them in their beaks to a suitable height and let them fall on to a rock, concrete seawall or other hard surface, when the shells are effectively cracked allowing the birds to enjoy the contents. The oystercatcher, or sea-pie, has a beak much resembling a knife which is perfectly adapted for opening all sorts of molluscs as well as stripping limpets from breakwaters and stones. A hundred years ago the fishermen of Furness and Ulverstone blamed the birds, and particularly the black-backed gulls, for carrying off large quantities of cockles when the beds were exposed at low tide.

At that time cockling was a staple industry in the area, evidence given before the Fisheries Inspectors in 1878 showing that whole families were engaged in it at Baycliff, Bardsey and Ulverstone, with many more at Flukeborough, Allithwaite, Cark and Silverdale. All told in the Morecambe Bay region there were more than a hundred carts out every day with six or seven people to each one. The cockles were sold at five or six shillings a box containing 70 quarts, about 30 going to a quart. Many of them went to Blackburn, Manchester, Bolton and Keighley, while the extent of the trade may be seen from the returns of the Furness Railway, the carriage of cockles from its various stations in 1877 being as follows: Barrow, 10 tons; Peel, 70; Dalton, 80; Askam, 220; Millom, 343; Ulverstone, 290; Cark, 1,160; Kent's Bank, 25; Arnside, 5; and Silverdale, 50. This makes a total of 2,253 tons worth about £5 a ton, but as at least a third more went for local consumption, the total value must have been around £14,000 a year.

There were many other districts where cockles were equally important but the method of gathering followed the same pattern, a group of people attached to one cart which they gradually filled by plying their rakes in the sandy mud. Another method was to stamp the feet thus bringing the cockles to the surface when they could be picked up. In some ways the cockle gatherers were more farmers than fishermen as they never went to sea and used only agricultural implements. Nevertheless, they played a useful part in the provision of valuable seafood and without them the shell-fish stalls would not have existed. Nor could they survive today without the few who still carry on the business, though their reduced numbers means that the price will never again be five or six shillings for 70 quarts.

Shrimps were much more highly esteemed and universally consumed in days gone by than they are now when the sight of a fishmonger's slab piled up with heaps of 'browns' and 'pinks' is something of a rarity. Their almost complete disappearance is not due to any shortage but to a change in public taste; with so many foods of convenience about, a fishmonger told me recently, people will not bother with them, they are too fiddling. If they have a mind for any they get foreign ones out of a tin already shelled. This attitude is reflected in places like Gravesend, Southwold and Great Yarmouth where hardly a boat is left to go out and catch them. Yet thirty or forty years ago they, along with many other areas like Harwich, Southend and all the centres round Morecambe Bay, sent trim little fleets to sea on every tide, especially in summer when all the visitors seemed to want shrimps for tea.

Supplies still reaching the markets are mostly caught, as they always have been, in trawl nets with a 9ft or 10ft beam and a fine-meshed cod-end. After being seived, or riddled, over the side, so that the undersized ones may escape, they are usually boiled on board, though at Great Yarmouth this was more often done ashore. A tell-tale whisp of smoke used to show when a shrimper had got his fire going and a boat engaged in this kind of fishing was not long in getting the name 'boiler'. Later this became 'bawley' in the East Anglian vernacular, hence bawley boat already referred to.

Sieves for culling shrimps were first employed at Leigh-on-Sea about 1830. The distance apart of the wires, called the gauge, is expressed in pennies, that is, the number of these coins placed face to face which will pass through. In the Thames fishing during June a threepenny seive was used but in winter this was exchanged for one with a guage of three half-pennies. The Rye and Lynn men, however, preferred fourpenny seives which of course meant much larger shrimps in the shops which met with a ready sale.

I expect most of us as children went shrimping with one of those little nets which were sold everywhere at seaside resorts, though my own catches I remember were meagre to say the least. A much larger version, often 4ft across, was used by the long-shoremen to get a gallon or two which they were only too glad to sell on the spot to holidaymakers. These 'push' nets were found wherever there was a sandy beach and when times were hard wives, sweethearts and children would often be seen, up to their armpits, shoving away to earn an extra shilling or two. Another method once common in many districts was to tow a beam trawl behind a horse and cart. A horse could go further out than a man and it was reckoned its hooves stirred up the shrimps when they were promptly caught in the net following behind. Paignton had a number of these horse dredges while several more operated from Broadsands. They were popular, too, at Friskney, on the Lincoln-shire side of the Wash, sometimes as many as thirty or forty being out at the same time. I was once on the beach somewhere near Noordwijk, in Holland, where horse trawling was going on, though it had been modernised in a very ingenious way. A small lorry, complete with steaming boiler, moved slowly along keeping level with the horse and when it came in to shake out the catch the lorry stopped, the shrimps were seived, plunged straight into the boiler and sold to bystanders within ten minutes of coming out of the sea. They, without a doubt, were the freshest shrimps I ever bought. A brief word about cooking them may not be amiss as most people make the mistake of boiling them too long which makes them tough and destroys the flavour. Take a good-sized saucepan of water and add a handful of kitchen salt; bring to the boil and put in the shrimps. The water will go off the boil for a minute or two but when it has boiled again continue for two minutes then pour through a colander and spread out the shrimps to dry on a large dish.

With the approach of autumn many of the Thames bawleys took their shrimp nets ashore and prepared for the sprat fishing. Come Guy Fawkes these delectable little fish were at their best and a pleasant childhood memory I have of the Fifth of November, apart from the bonfires and the fireworks, is the great dish of them my mother always had ready for our supper just as the last rocket had sped up into the darkness. For a youngster it was a great treat not having to use a knife and fork; like asparagus I was allowed to eat them with my fingers and that was much more fun, holding them by head and tail and nibbling off the flesh from the backbone. I have never since eaten sprats in any other way.

They were caught in two ways, by drifting, as for herring, but using a smaller-meshed net, and by a massive, funnel-shaped device called a stow-net, the management of which is clearly shown in the sketch. The mouth of the net was kept open by two beams attached to the anchor cable by bridles, the upper one being suspended port and starboard of the vessel's bows by two ropes, called 'templines'. The lower beam could be lifted up to close the net by a 'wind chain' brought to the windlass, the anchor cable being turned up on bitts. A further rope, known as a 'pinion', was attached to the cod-end where the fish collected, which was hauled in when the net was to be emptied. A scythe-shaped instrument called a 'mingle' divided off about three bushels, the cod-end was brought on board and the contents emptied into the hold. This was repeated till the net was clear when fishing would be resumed. (See page 156.)

The Leigh boats usually worked in company, three men to a boat, the fastest sailer acting as carrier to get the combined catch to market as quickly as possible. When plenty of fish were about deliveries were made to the carrier by skiff but if things were quiet boats would wait for her to come by so that she could take the catch straight into her own hold, thus saving unnecessary handling. They were often out for a week at a stretch and generally had enough provisions to last them that time, consisting

L

mainly of bread, cheese, butter, flour, currants, tea and coffee besides coal and oil.

Stow-boating was also carried on in the Solent and Robert C. Leslie, that very competent observer with brush and pen of sea life a hundred years ago, writes of these vessels and their gear in his *Sea-Painter's Log*, published in 1886. Telling of one fitting out, he says: 'As the tide flows and the vessel floats again, the long, brown, funnel-shaped net is carefully taken over her side and triced up in the rigging to air. The small mesh of the stow-net, only half an inch from knot to knot in parts, gives it a very solid look when so hanging, quite distinguishing it from the trawler's nets. Then the upper and lower beams, spars some 30ft. long, together with a strange-looking, long-limbed anchor and many fathoms of stout rope-cable, are taken on board. This anchor will often have to hold both net and vessel against strong tides, wind and sea; the net riding to it, mouth to tide, nearly under the vessel's bottom... When open, the mouth has a gape of some 900sq. ft. . . Strange to say, spratters, especially in rough weather, rather dread getting the net full of fish. It floats as long as there is life in the fish but must be at once swept and slung by many ropes alongside, for should it sink it may be impossible to raise it again. At such times a full net has often to be cut across in several places to start the fish out of it, so enabling the men, by throwing away some tons of fish, to save their net and the rest of the catch. A net full would weigh out of water eighty or ninety tons, while the whole capacity of the stow-boat is seldom much over thirty tons.' Unfortunately, only a proportion of this plenty ever reached the market, let alone the poor man's table, for close at hand there was always the farmer with his tumbril anxious to carry off all he could get. Very often the carriers bound for London would be held up by fog or bad weather and be forced to put into places like Sheerness, Gravesend or Erith and sell their sprats for next to nothing. Rotting and stinking the farmers would cart them away more often than not to be spread over the Kentish hop-gardens.

The smallest longshore fish of all is undoubtedly the whitebait, though it is not a distinct species but the fry of many different kinds which congregate in shoals during warm weather, mainly along the shores of estuaries and in the lower reaches of big rivers. Before the Thames was a sewer, whitebait swam as far up as London Bridge; in the illustration, dated 1837, two boatmen

Peter netting in the Upper Pool, London

are seen peter-netting, or seining, for whitebait in the Upper Pool, a demonstration of how clean the river was then. The sailing vessels, mostly coasters, massed on either bank, make an interesting comparison with the paddle-steamer coming up with the tide, bound from Woolwich to Hungerford market.

Frank Buckland established, by personal observation, that in an average sample of whitebait there might be found the fry of no less than eleven kinds of fish, comprised as follows: herrings, sprats, gobies, weevers, sand-eels, smelts, pipe-fish, sticklebacks, brown shrimps, red shrimps and gorebills, sometimes called gar-pike. The whitebait as an item of diet was unknown before about 1780 when a Blackwall fisherman, Richard Cannon, first brought them to the notice of tavern keepers in that place and Greenwich. Besides the Thames they were once plentiful in the Medway and were fished for extensively by the men of Rochester and Queenborough. Nowadays, owing to pollution, they seldom come further than the Lower Hope, but whitebait fishing on any scale is just about extinct. As we have seen in the illustration of the Upper Pool, they were caught with seine nets, of very fine mesh, and by stow-boating, when the top beam would be only a foot or two down, whitebait being surface swimmers.

For any one lucky enough to obtain a supply of them and being doubtful about how they should be cooked, let me quote from Pennant's *British Zoology, 1776*. 'During the month of July,' he says, 'there appear in the Thames near Blackwall and Greenwich innumerable multitudes of small fish which are known to the Londoners by the name of whitebait. They are esteemed very delicious when fried with fine flour and occasion, during the season, a vast resort of the lower order of epicures to the taverns contiguous to the places they are taken at.' Tastes must have changed later on for an old Queenborough longshoreman, who started fishing about the time of Waterloo, told Frank Buckland that 'whitebait was never poor man's food, the poor people would not give it belly room'. But monarchs, noblemen and lord mayors certainly did and few royal banquets or formal dinners would have been complete without it. By 1880 it had become rather expensive fare retailing at about a shilling a pound, the same price as beef; and beef, except in the form of marrow bones for stock, was largely beyond the pockets of the poor.

However, in London at least, there was a highly-prized alternative, the ubiquitous eel. It was turned into pies, stewed, broiled but above all jellied, in which form it became almost a national dish. The cries of the costermongers and hawkers which used to echo round the streets of London bear testimony to the popular demand: 'Buy My Dish of Great Eeles!'—'Hot Eele Pyes'—'Large Silver Eeles, a Groat a Pound, Live Eeles'—'Who's for an Eele Pye?' Many of them came from the upper reaches of the Thames where they were caught in fyke-nets, long, tubular contrivances of fine netting, usually set by weirs and mill-streams. A great many, too, arrived in vans, and later by rail, from the Norfolk broads where many of the marshmen had 'setts'. A sett consisted of a close-meshed net the bottom of which was weighted and rested on the river bed while the top was buoyed with corks to keep it on the surface. Worked into it were several openings which formed the mouths of circular, bag-like nets, called 'pods'. Blocks and tackle allowed the corked rope to be hauled down to the river bottom, where it remained during the day so as not to interfere with passing craft, and up again to the surface at night when most of the fishing was done. When the eels struck this wall of netting they tried to find a way round it and eventually ended up in the pods from which it was impossible for them to escape. Some remarkable 'takes' have been recorded by this simple but very effective method, one man at Fishley, on the Bure, having landed 110 stones for a single night's fishing. Another, at Hardley Cross on the Yare, netted 300 stones in four nights.

Breydon Water, that wild and lovely spot at the back of Great Yarmouth, once nurtured what Arthur Patterson described as 'a semi-amphibious fraternity' which, with boats, nets and guns, earned a livelihood there all the year round. Mullet, flounders, salmon trout, eels and even sturgeon were found there, but though these provided good catches at times it was the smelt fishing, done mostly on the Burgh flats hard by the Roman castle, that gave the most regular employment. It was mainly an autumn and winter fishery carried on with drag-nets about 80yd long, almost the same as those used on the coast for taking salmon trout, but with about fifty meshes to the yard. A remarkable characteristic of the smelt is that when freshly caught it has a distinct and unmistakable smell of cucumber. This disappears on cooking, which may be done by dusting with flour and lightly frying in fresh dairy butter. Like the whitebait they once found great favour on London dinner tables and were fished for in many places besides the Norwich river, in the Solway Firth, at Ulverstone, in the Wash with boats from Boston and Lynn taking part, and along the south coast where Brighton was the most important centre.

I have called this chapter 'A Pretty Kettle of Fish' because in somewhat disordered fashion it has, perforce, dealt with a variety of fish and subjects. Dictionaries, while fairly unanimous in defining the meaning of this expression as 'an awkward mess or situation', are not very forthcoming as to its origin. My own belief is that it came into use during the seventeenth or eighteenth century when 'engines' called kettle-nets were established all round our coasts. What they looked like and how they worked may be seen from the illustration of one that was still in operation on the Essex side of the Thames about eighty years ago. The tide has ebbed uncovering the flats though it is not yet quite low water, and two men, one leading a horse and cart, the other with a scoop net on his shoulder, prepare to remove the catch. Fish may be seen splashing about on the right of the circular pocket, where the water is still fairly deep. As the tide began to go out they swam with it over the flats until they met the barrier which stretches away to the left almost up to the shore. When meeting an obstruction of this kind fish instinctively turn seaward and in this case, by so doing, they were directed down into the pocket, or 'kettle'. It was an unselective method and when the water has receded sufficiently for the men to get into it, the kettle may be found to have captured flounders, plaice, dabs, soles, codling, salmon trout, skate, whiting, bass, mullet or, indeed, just about anything that swims. They will all have to be sorted out and put into different baskets before they can be sold and it is easy enough to imagine one saying to the other as they survey the task, 'Thas a perty kettle o' fish we got today and no mistake'. Unlike drifting, trawling or lining, kettle-netting was conducted where any one so inclined could go along and watch, and no doubt at times considerable numbers gathered to see the catch taken up. Such an expression, therefore, would not long have remained just fishermen's talk but would eventually have been used by all and sundry. (See page 156.)

Another unselective mode of fishing was with the trammel net. We tend to use the word today more in its negative form, ie., untrammelled progress, meaning to get along without hindrance. Fish, however, when encountering this formidable device, made very little further progress. A trammel really comprised three nets in one set on to a back rope, which was corked, and a foot rope weighted with lead, heavy enough to keep on the bottom, the buoyancy of the corks maintaining the net in a more or less vertical position. It was anchored at each end and usually shot with the tide and not across it. The middle one of the three nets, called the 'inner wall', was 3–4in mesh, and on either side of it were two 'outer walls' of 17–19in mesh. Length varied from 30yd to 100yd but the depth was never more than 2yd, experience showing that this was sufficient for catching mullet, soles, plaice, crawfish, crabs and lobsters, which generally made up the bulk of the catch.

Fish swimming or crawling along the seabed would pass without difficulty through the large-meshed outer wall, encounter the small-meshed inner, which they would carry far enough to go past the second outer, the mesh of which would then pull tight behind them forming a pocket difficult, if not impossible, to get out of. One great advantage of the trammel was that it could be shot and left while some other kind of fishing, like hand lining, was carried on. They are not entirely obsolete, the men of Selsey still working them from time to time, while in France some years ago they were in use along the banks of the Gironde.

Such, then, were some of the many ingenious ways by which our forefathers caught their fish and gained a modest livelihood, ways born out of generations of experience and perfected, no doubt, by a long process of trial and error. Their aim was not to savage and exploit the seas, as we do now, but to work their boats and gear according to the season so that prime, fresh fish always went into the housewife's basket. In the main they were rough, unlettered men, but hardy, wise in the ways of the sea and, above all, proud of their calling. Through them, too, ran a rich seam of simple philosophy summed up, perhaps, by some words spoken by one of them to his mate as they cleaned their nets of some fine, full herrings: 'If God were to send 'is bill for all them fish as we've took from th' sea, I reckons as 'ow we'd never be able to pay it.'

The younger generation of longshoremen seem, on the surface, to be a slightly different breed, perhaps because they go down to their boats on four wheels instead of two feet and have a transistor tucked away under the sternsheets, 'just to get the weather', as they will tell you. But though they use engines instead of sails, and pot-haulers to save back-breaking toil, find the fish with echo-sounders and have tractors to heave their boats up the beach, at heart they are much the same as their ancestors; but they admit the job is easier now than it used to be. There is amongst these younger men a marked spirit of independence which has come about, I think, because they get good money for what they catch and have never had to suffer the hand-to-mouth existence which all too often was the lot of their fathers. This admirable self-reliance is all to the good and augurs well for the future of longshoring.

So, having caught our fish, as Mrs Beeton might say, we can, if we wish, cook it and eat it without more ado. But perhaps we may pause a while yet to spin a few yarns, consider some curious recipes and discover a little about the gentle art of curing.

CHAPTER NINE

# Fire-Flair Oil, Brine and Smoke

You never knew with Trouncer when he was pulling your leg; to be generous, I think one might say that after his third or fourth pint he tended to embellish his tales a little. And being well past the allotted span of three score years and ten, most of which he had spent on the North Sea, was probably like Somerset Maugham in later life, who admitted being unable to distinguish what was fact and what was fiction in many of his stories. On this occasion Trouncer had been questioned by one of the younger fishermen with the rather challenging words, 'I hev heard tell as 'ow yew're supposed t' hev seen a sea sarpint once; is thet a fac' now?'

The five or six of us gathered in the snug bar of that windswept pub looked expectantly in his direction and saw him fix his interrogator with a steely eye. 'Supposed?' he said, 'what d'yer mean supposed? 'Course I see 'un. Th' wonder bein' as 'ow I'm 'ere t' speak on 't, seein's I was near devoured by th' crittur.'

"Ow was thet, then,' said one of the company, 'were yew orf in yer boat?'

'Thet I were, bor, 'bout a mile, bit sou' o' th' 'arbour, 'anging on t' me 'errin' nets, so I cudn't move nor dew nothin'.' Trouncer looked regretfully at his empty mug and when it had been replenished, with a murmured 'Thank 'e', someone said he didn't hold with sea serpents, reckoned they were all imagination.

'Oh, yew dew, dew yew? Well, if yew'd bin along o' me thet day, yew wudn't 'a' called 't imaginashun. But as yew weren't, I'll tell 'ow 't come about.' Taking a long, appreciative swig and stuffing some shag into his clay, Trouncer embarked on his yarn.

He told us how he had gone off alone just before first light to see if he could pin a few herring; his mate, being a bit poorly, stayed ashore. The day broke fine and clear with hardly a breath of wind and as he rode comfortably to his nets felt a bite of bread and cheese and a drink of tea from his bottle would not come amiss.

'I'd jest put th' bottle t' me lips,' he went on, 'when sudden like, 'twixt me an' th' land, there were a stirrin' up o' th' water, then out o' 't slowly rose a fearsome grit 'ead, wi' a snout like a pig, two huge eyes, what began peerin' at me, an' a long neck wi' stragglin' 'airs down th' back, what a 'orse might 'ave. Me innards they turned t' jelly bein' terryfied as I were th' beast wud come for me. But thank God 't didn't, though I'd got th' tiller in me 'and by this time t' gi' 't a crack if 't 'ad o' done, but I doubt a monster thet size wudn't o' took much notice, an' thas th' truth.'

'What did 't dew, then?' someone asked.

'Started t' swim, if thet's what yew can call 't, away t' th' norrard, 'umping 'ts body into arches like a grit snake as 't went, an' a more 'orrid sight I never want t' see. Arter goin' 'bout a quarter o' a mile, swingin' 'ts 'ead right an' left all th' time as if 't weren't sure where 't were, 't seemed t' let 'tself sink, an' thet were th' end o' 't. But I don't mind tellin' on yer, I 'auled me nets an skidaddled back t' 'arbour like greased lightin'.'

Naturally, there followed some lively discussion about sea serpents in general and Trouncer's in particular, when young Billy, who had started the whole thing, asked, "Ow many 'umps dew yew reckon as 'ow 't 'ad when 't started swimmin' orf?'

'Three,' replied Trouncer, without hesitation, 'an' if someone'll gi' me a bit o' paper an' pencil, I'll draw th' bloomin' thing jest 'ow 't were.'

The landlord obligingly produced these two items and for the next ten minutes Trouncer was occupied with his drawing. Satisfied at last, he pushed it away from him, and laying down the pencil took up his mug. 'Thas jest as I see 'un,' he said, 'wi' all them scales runnin' th' whole length o' 'im. See 'em clear, I cud, bein' no more'n fifty yards away from 'im.'

It was a remarkably good sketch which showed all the details he had mentioned. The head was raised some six or eight feet,

two prominent ears extended upwards from behind the eyes,
which were large and seemed to protrude slightly. Behind was the
body of the thing, covered with scales, and forming three semi-
circular humps. Round what I suppose might be called its chest,
Trouncer had drawn the suggestion of a bow-wave to show it was
moving. In the background was the coastline with all its familiar
landmarks, but what struck me most was that in the last arch, the
hump forming a kind of frame for it, was a sketch, quite unmistakable, of Walberswick church tower.

I pointed to it and asked Trouncer what made him put it in.

'What made me?' he repeated, 'because thet's 'ow it were when
I seed 't. Clear as a pikestaff. Remember 't now, as if 't were
yesterday, seein' th' old church wi' thet there crittur's body sort o'
arched over 't.'

I thought at the time, and I think now, that a fleeting impression of that kind might well be photographed on the mind, a small
detail one would not easily forget nor, for that matter, be able to
invent. Which is not to say we swallowed Trouncer's yarn without
a pinch of salt. But there had been several reports about that time,
some forty years ago, of so-called sea serpents being seen off the
Norfolk and Suffolk coast and we were all prepared to give
Trouncer the benefit of the doubt to the extent that he might have
seen 'something', though we remained sceptical about its being a
real, live sea serpent. These reported sightings, I think, originated
in the passage of large flocks of scoter duck which are dark in
colour and fly in a long, undulating line only a foot or so above the
water. Seen from a distance they can easily be mistaken for a
large, snake-like object, travelling on the surface at considerable
speed. Fishing single-handed in a small boat I have had them pass
me at no more than thirty or forty yards and at first glance I
wondered if I was 'seeing things'.

Quite apart from monsters, real or imagined, there is plenty
going on in the sea at night which now and again makes you think
your senses are playing tricks. I remember being off Benacre Ness
one very still night with my young son trying for a few herring,
when we were startled by a succession of eerie grunts and snorts
quite close to us. We looked all round trying hard to see where

they came from and at last noticed several gleams of phosphorescence in the water, following each other along the nets, which we were lying to, then past the boat and away out to sea. Two dorsal fins broke the surface as they went by us and my youngster said, 'Porpoises, I think, Dad'. And porpoises they proved to be. Having encountered our nets as they swam along the shore, they immediately turned seaward to find a way round, and once clear of the boat we could see them swing slowly to the northward and resume their course. On another occasion, in almost the same position, we were hauling the nets when there was a commotion two or three feet below the surface, quite different from the usual surging about of the fish. To our astonishment we found a guillemot, which had obviously been diving near the nets trying to steal some fish, with its neck caught in the meshes. We carefully disentangled the bird and lay it on the floor boards where it flapped around looking very dazed. It could only have got into the net as we were hauling otherwise it would have been drowned as guillemots, like other diving birds, can stay under water only for a short time before having to come up for air. However, after a few moments our strange capture had recovered enough to stand, and when eventually we picked it up and returned it to the water, it paddled off apparently none the worse for its experience.

Many years ago some fishermen were rowing over Breydon Water bound for Burgh flats to drag for smelts. In the fading daylight and gathering haze they noticed what they thought was a bush floating up on the tide, but which on closer inspection they made out to be a sturgeon resting on the surface. With a running noose on the end of one of their lines they pulled quietly up and managed to slip it over the tail, when the fish at once made off and succeeded in freeing itself. But it did not go far and when once more it came to rest they made a second attempt, the sturgeon this time dashing away and towing the boat with it. After a hundred yards they were able to haul the great fish alongside and stun it with an iron bar, when a struggle followed to heave it on board; not really surprising for when it was taken back to Yarmouth and weighed it tipped the scales at a little over 160lb.

When there were few mechanical aids for launching and hauling up beach boats horses were often called upon to assist, the
south landing at Flamborough being one place where they were
commonly employed. One might think, however, that dogs could
play little part in this heavy sort of work, yet there were two
villages on the Devonshire coast, Hallsands and Beesands, where
labradors often helped the fishermen ashore. They were trained
to swim off as the boats neared the beach, take a piece of wood
in their mouths to which a light line was attached, then swim back
pulling it with them. Those waiting ashore seized the line, the
crew bent on a rope, and when this had been hauled in they
waited for a 'smooth', took the next oncoming wave and ran the
boats high and dry on to the beach. The sturdy work of these dogs
often allowed boats to get in when it would have been dangerous,
if not impossible, without them. Homing pigeons, too, were
pressed into service on the east coast of Scotland during the
herring season, though their work was less strenuous. Some of
the curers, who were also pigeon fanciers, sent a basket of two or
three away in the boats and when daylight came, with the nets
hauled and the catch determined, the skipper would write the
number of barrels on a piece of paper, attach it to a pigeon's leg
and release it. The bird arrived back well before the boat enabling
the curer to know in advance how many fish he had to deal with
and to plan accordingly.

I have avoided any reference to the hazards and dangers of
fishing because they are too apparent to merit much comment in
a work of this nature. In the past, however, comparison was often
made between the risks run by fishermen and miners, the two
occupations generally regarded as being prone to serious accidents. Some interesting figures are available for the years 1880–
1–2 when a total of 80,000 men were employed in the fishing
fleets and the number of deaths amounted to 880, an average of
293 per annum. The mortality rate was thus 3.66 per 1,000,
whereas mining, from 1870–80, had a corresponding rate of 2.3
per 1,000. Stated in another way, one life was lost for every 1,435
tons of fish landed in one year, and one miner's life was lost for
every 128,274 tons of coal brought to the surface in one year.

Besides the hardship, damage and loss of gear suffered through bad weather, fishermen often sustained personal injury when handling their catches. Longshoremen in particular were always on their guard against a small, yellow-coloured fish called a weever, the neck spines and gill-cover spines of which have poison glands. Numbers of them were found in nearly every haul of shrimps, each one being carefully picked out, trodden on and put over the side. Inevitably, some were not seen in time and the fingers would be pierced by the venomous spines, causing an excruciating, stinging pain, followed usually by swelling and numbness that could last for several days. When the bawley boatmen were stung they plunged their fingers into the boiling brine prepared for the shrimps, though such a remedy must have been more painful than the complaint. Others would rub the affected part with grease or turpentine, if any was handy, at the same time putting a tourniquet of cod line round finger or wrist to prevent the trouble spreading. Still others favoured cutting the liver out of the offending fish and rubbing it on the wound, the oil acting as an emollient.

So frequently were the shrimpers of Leigh-on-Sea stung by weevers that they sought medical advice and were advised to have with them at all times when afloat a bottle of olive oil with a little opium in it. It was to be applied with gentle friction after which a woollen stocking, steeped in water as hot as could be borne, was to be wrapped round hand and wrist. This had to be repeated at intervals after returning ashore, though poultices of poppy-heads or linseed oil with a sprinkling of laudanum, were equally efficacious.

Dog-fish could also prove nasty customers possessing a spike on their backs quite capable of piercing a sea-boot and penetrating into the foot or leg, though it was a straightforward wound, no poison being injected. When long lining the first dog-fish caught usually had its throat cut, the blood thus shed being intended as a warning to others of its kind to stay away from the hooks. An even more unpleasant specimen was the sting-ray which has a lethal barb, 5–7in long, protruding rearwards from above the base of the tail. In the Thames estuary they were commonly termed 'fire-slowers', no doubt a corruption of the more generally accepted 'fire-flair', of which Oppian wrote:

> The Fire-flair's tail its venom'd shaft contains;
> Nor time, nor waste the poisonous treasure drains.
> Murderous alike they ravage all the sea,
> First give the mortal wound, then seize the prey.

I have come across no specific cure for injuries inflicted by the sting-ray which consist of lacerated flesh quickly followed by violent inflammation. However, fishermen's wives years ago used to boil down their livers, the resulting oil being regarded as a panacea for burns, pains and bruises. Rubbed into sea-boots it was said to keep them black and soft. A fish, 2ft long, excluding the tail, would produce half a gallon of oil. Dog-fish livers were similarly treated though this oil was kept for dressing sails. A belief long held in many fishing villages was that flounder's blood, taken on a lump of sugar, was a sure prophylactic and cure for whooping cough.

If whitebait were the smallest fish sought by longshoremen, then certainly the biggest were the basking sharks, found in early summer off the west coast of Ireland during their northward migration. As many as a hundred at a time were frequently sighted off Tory Island and the shores of Donegal, resting on the surface enjoying the sunshine, their large dorsal fins rising 3–4ft out of the water. They were harpooned from boats in much the same way as whales and were taken for the oil contained in their livers. Often measuring 30ft in length, a single liver could weigh 2 tons and make enough oil to fill 6–8 barrels of a quality equal to that of the finest spermaceti. Unlike the whale there was no blubber between the skin and the flesh, so after the stomach had been split down and the liver extracted, the carcase was set adrift. There was a superstition that to bring it anywhere near the shore would drive away all the other sharks.

The making of fires and the application of heat in one form or another was very much a part of the longshoremen's life. Besides the boiling down of oil just mentioned there was hot tar to be prepared for the boats, cutch for the sails and nets, very often linseed for the long lines. Above all, fires were needed for the smoking of fish, though they had to be of a kind to produce as little heat as possible. Sawdust answered best for this purpose as it smouldered, caused the maximum amount of smoke, seldom burst into flame and burnt for a long time. Oak, elm, ash and similar hardwoods eventually became recognised as the most suitable for fish smoking on account of the flavour they imparted. Pine and other coniferous varieties were avoided as they produced an unpleasant, resinous taste. Turf, or peat, will always be associated with the Scottish village of Findon where it was used to smoke the once-famous Finnan haddocks.

The original object of treating fish in this way was to preserve them, a process aided by the salting they received beforehand. This was done either by immersion in strong brine for a given period or by covering and rousing in dry salt. In time preserving became of secondary importance as cured and smoked fish attained their rightful place at table as a palatable and very acceptable dish. Since the war, unfortunately, there has been a marked deterioration in the quality of all smoked fish, the present-day bloater, for instance, being rarely worth the eating. To overcome this I built a small smoke-house at the end of the garden to produce bloaters, kippers, haddocks and the like in the traditional way and with the old-time flavour. In this I was helped by having the sea on my doorstep to provide fresh fish and a timber mill not far up the road with as much oak sawdust as I cared to take away.

A structure like this is very easy to make. The base, or hearth, comprises five courses of brick, 27in wide and 18in deep, on top of which is placed a wooden frame clad with $\frac{1}{2}$in boards, the front section being detachable. A piece of aquaply, set at a slight angle, serves for roof, a space of about an inch being left between it and the sides to give ventilation without allowing the smoke to escape too quickly. The whole thing stands about 8ft high and friends are in the habit of referring to it as my sentry box which, indeed, it rather resembles. Notched battens screwed to the sides take the spits, or rods, which carry the herring, being placed right at the top under the roof. For sprats suitable lengths of heavy galvanised wire serve admirably, while a couple of frames, made to lodge on the battens, and covered with small-mesh wire-netting, accommodate fillets which have to be laid flat. Pieces of 1in sq wood, the same length as the spits, have wire nails driven in on opposite sides and the heads chopped off, to make what are called tenterhooks for hanging herring after they have been split. In this guise they become kippers. In the roof itself are several hooks to hang legs and sides of pork, for once you have a smoke-house, if only a small one, it is quite easy to do your own Christmas hams, home-cured bacon and that popular Dutch dish, smoked beef.

In order to produce as much smoke as possible but without flame and consequently the minimum of heat, only a very small vent is needed in the brick base to provide sufficient draught. I started by drilling a hole in the mortar between two bricks and gradually enlarged it till I found enough air coming through to keep the sawdust smouldering. When kindling a fire I crumple up three or four sheets of newspaper and press them down gently on the floor of the hearth; then comes a generous sprinkling of shavings, which can be of any kind of wood and not necessarily oak; finally I sift on a layer of sawdust about two inches thick, smoothing it out to ensure even burning. With this arrangement the newspaper ignites the shavings which in turn gives a start to the sawdust, at the same time allowing air to get underneath and preventing the sawdust from forming a solid heap, when it usually goes out. If all goes well it will burn for about five hours without attention and I usually contrive to start smoking about tea-time then build a second fire just before going to bed. This gives the fish two or three hours to dry off in the cool should they be required for breakfast, as they often are.

The popularity of the peat-smoked Finnan haddock led to many imitations wherever this fish was available and one of the most successful was the so-called London haddock. The ever wideawake costermongers soon realised the possibilities of this trade with Billingsgate on their doorsteps and backyards where they could salt and smoke, though the conditions where this work was done were primitive, to say the least. Frank Buckland, in 1873, quoted an eye-witness account from the periodical *Land*

M

*and Water* which gives a good idea of how this business was conducted.

'The curing of haddock for the London market,' writes the author, 'is chiefly carried on by the costermongers on the Surrey side of the river Thames, in the neighbourhood of Camberwell. The tenements generally have a yard at the back and emerging from the passage I find myself in a small railed enclosure redolent of fish-like perfumes and ranged around close to the rails are tubs, pans and, I may say, vessels of all descriptions filled with a fluid of a yellow colour and of an oily consistence. This, I am informed, is the "pickle", a solution of salt and water. Occupying one corner stands a sort of sentry-box, the curing house. It is composed of scraps of plank, staves of casks, fragments of oil-cloth and old rags for caulking. Numerous ledges are nailed along two of its sides. The haddocks are brought into the enclosure and boys and girls at once commence removing the heads, split them open, scrape off all the dirt and plunge them into the pickling tubs according to size. The fish soak in the pickle for about three hours and then the skewering-up process commences.

'The larger haddocks are first one by one taken from the tubs and a peeled rod is passed through each fish until there are as many as the rod will contain, the ends are laid upon the lowermost ledges in rows until filled up and so on until the smallest are on the top ledges. A fire is kindled on the ground which is kept smouldering by the judicious application of sawdust underneath the haddocks. The curing-house is closely shut up and when the haddocks are sufficiently tinged of a yellow colour they are considered to be cured. From six to eight hours is quite sufficient to enable a skilled curer to split, salt and smoke a load of haddocks fit for sale.'

Henry Mayhew, in *London Labour and the London Poor*, published in 1851, describes even cruder methods of producing smoked haddocks which, nevertheless, seemed to find a ready sale. One costermonger he was on good terms with admitted to him that 'there's Scotch haddies that never knew anything about Scotland, for I've made lots of them myself by Tower Street, just a jump or two from Lambeth station-house. I used to make them

on Sundays. I was a wet-fish seller then and when I couldn't get
through my haddocks or my whitings of a Saturday night, I wasn't
going to give them away to folks that wouldn't take the trouble to
lift me out of a gutter if I fell there, so I preserved them. I've
made haddies of whitings, and good ones too, and Joe made them
of codlings besides. I had a bit of a back-yard to two rooms, one
over the other, that I had then, and on a Sunday I set some wet
wood a-fire and put it under a great tub. My children used to gut
and wash the fish and I hung them on hooks all round the sides
of the tub, and made a bit of a chimney in a corner of the top of
the tub, and in that way I gave them a jolly good smoking. My
wife had a dry-fish stall and sold them and used to sing out "Real
Scotch haddies" and tell people how they was from Aberdeen;
I've often been fit to laugh she did it so clever.

'I had a way of giving them a yellow colour like the real Scotch,
but that's a secret. After they was well smoked they was hung up
to dry all round the room we lived in. There's more ways than one
of making 6d. if a man has eyes in his head and keeps them open.
Haddocks that wouldn't fetch 1d. a piece, nor any money at all,
of a Saturday night, I've sold—at least she has (indicating his
wife by a motion of his thumb)—at 2d., 3d. and 4d. I've bought
fish of costers that was over on a Saturday night to make Scotch
haddies of them. I've tried experiments, too. Ivy burnt under
them gave them, I thought, a nice sort of flavour, rather peppery,
for I used always to taste them. Ivy with brown berries on it I
liked best. Holly wasn't no good. A black-currant bush was, but
it's too dear; and, indeed, it couldn't be had. I mostly spread
wetted fire-wood, as green as could be got, or damp sticks of any
kind, over shavings, and kept feeding the fire. Sometimes I burnt
sawdust. Somehow,' he concludes, 'the dry-fish trade fell off.
People does get so prying and so knowing there's no doing nothing
now.'

Which is not really surprising for the 'haddies' produced by
this cockney sparrow must have been quite horrible. By burning
green wood he made more steam than smoke, a fatal mistake,
calculated to turn the fish limp and soggy. Being stale, too, and
probably tainted before they went into the brine, one can only

think that the people who bought them must have been extremely gullible or had never tasted a genuine, peat-smoked Finnan. His dodge for giving them the authentic yellow tinge was simply the addition of a handful of dye, possibly saffron, to the brine, and it is from such shady beginnings that the present-day practice of colouring fish before smoking has grown up. I must confess I have never tried ivy, holly or blackcurrant bushes and imagine they were only pressed into service because they could be grubbed up nearby. If I did they would have to be cut and dried for at least a year to get the sap out of them. It is so important to avoid all trace of steam when smoking that every bag of fresh sawdust I get from the mill is spread out and allowed to dry thoroughly before being used. This ensures, too, that the fire will burn right through and not have to be continually re-lit.

While curers favour oak, elm and ash in preference to other kinds of wood because of the fine, rich flavour they impart to the fish, no one with a smoke-house need necessarily limit himself to these varieties nor be content with wood alone. For instance, there is no problem in producing excellent imitation Finnan haddocks if you buy a small bag of garden peat, let it dry out completely, and burn it just like sawdust over a bed of newspapers crumpled up and shavings. Two or three hours in strong brine and about five hours in this kind of smoke makes a dish that will grace any table. Quite recently I was in the New Forest and came across some gorse bushes which had been uprooted and were destined ere long for the bonfire. I rescued a number of branches and eventually used them in small billets to smoke some bass. The result was most interesting as a suggestion of that peculiarly pleasant tang associated with gorse in bloom seemed to get into the fish. The value of juniper, added to the oak, has long been recognised in the smoking of salmon because of the slight aromatic flavour it gives, while a few shivers of hickory left to smoulder on top of the sawdust add a nutty taste to cod fillets and suchlike.

There is no reason either why anyone with a smoke-house should confine himself to producing only bloaters, kippers and haddocks, the most commonly cured fish. Sprats are very simple to do, as are eels, though these need a good twenty-four hours in the smoke, and mackerel, even horse-mackerel, split like kippers and well salted, need to hang for only four or five hours. Slightly more troublesome are cods' roes, usually at their best in January and February. They need smothering in salt for about six hours, then washing and being allowed to dry, after which they may be laid out on the wire racks and the fire started. Here again a lot of smoking is necessary as they are thick and compact and it has seldom taken me less than a day and a half to turn out nice, firm specimens. The fresh-water angler need not be forgotten, either, for smoked trout, prepared in much the same way as bloaters, eat better, in my opinion, than when they are fresh.

Many a skill went to the making of an old-time longshoreman; he was in turn sailor, fisherman, bait-gatherer, net-braider, ship-wright, sail-maker, often his own salesman, more often still the curer of the fish he caught. He never flaunted these skills but he was proud of them. His attitude was admirably, if curiously, expressed on a scrawled sign that used to be displayed in Gorleston—Fresh Boiled Shrimps Caught By The Catcher. What he intended customers to understand was that he had taken his boat out of the harbour at three o'clock that morning, single-handed, sailed into Yarmouth Roads, trawled up and down for five or six hours, mended his net a couple of times after it had been rent on some wreckage or an old anchor, riddled his shrimps after picking out all the weevers, star-fish, miller's thumbs, weed and other rubbish, returned to harbour, carried his catch home, filled the boiler with water from the pump, lit a fire, put half a gallon or so of shrimps into innumerable small bags of netting, boiled each one and spread their contents on trays to dry, with measures and paper bags handy—all ready for the visitors as they wandered leisurely down to the beach after breakfast.

No longshoreman ever 'took' to the sea, he was born to it, just as he was to all the other skills of his trade which, from a child, he saw going on around him every day. As one of them said to me, 'Why, lor', I don't never recollect not bein' able t' braid a net, an' thas a fac'.' He could have said the same about fashioning a new spar, cutching sails, setting up a trawl-net or baiting long lines. He began learning these things from the time when he struggled down to the beach clutching his mother's skirt. At six, probably, he made his first trip, at eight or nine he pulled an oar, at ten he took the tiller. By eleven or twelve he was 'the boy' serving as mate with father, uncle or brother, and by sixteen, like as not, was skipper of his own boat. When other boys, in other trades, were beginning their apprenticeships, the longshore lad was out of his time, already a skilled man, helping to support the family. Leading no textbook life he had little cause to regret his scanty education which at least taught him 'to figure', read and, above all, sing hymns. Without being ostentatiously religious he was devout and sincere in his beliefs and the church or chapel he gazed on during the week when out at sea plying nets and lines, usually saw him and his family in their seats on a Sunday. The gruff yet fervent voice which chanted hymns joined with equal gusto in such tavern ditties as 'Trawler Boy', 'I'm Jolly Jack the Sailor Lad' or 'Farewell, farewell My Own True Love', when of a Saturday night there were pints all round and someone with a concertina, melodeon or fiddle was generally on hand to provide the accompaniment whether for song or dance. The 'stepping' of these fishermen was a joy to watch and when the wives were persuaded to hitch their skirts and join in it was rare entertainment.

The poet Crabbe who lived cheek by jowl with the longshoremen of Aldeburgh in the latter half of the eighteenth century had little liking for them or their way of life—

'Here joyless roam a wild amphibious race,
With sullen woe displayed on every face;
Who, far from civil arts and social fly,
And scowl at strangers with suspicious eye.'

After making much of their smuggling activities, common enough then round all the coasts of Britain, he denounces them as wreckers and goes on to describe how they

'Wait on the shore and, as the waves run high,
On the toss'd vessel bend their eager eye;
Which to their coast directs its vent'rous way,
Theirs, or the ocean's, miserable prey.'

It is true enough that this sort of thing did go on when times were bad the men of Leigh-on-Sea, Southend and Whitstable not even being content to 'wait on the shore'. They preferred dropping down to the Maplins when a northerly blow looked imminent and as darkness came on hoisting lights in their rigging with the aim of leading London-bound colliers or timber barques on to the sands. When successful they innocently approached the stranded vessels with offers of assistance, such as laying out anchors and helping to lighten them by throwing much of their cargo over the side. They were well paid for these 'services' and in addition reaped a good harvest from the jettisoned goods they later salvaged.

The beachmen of Great Yarmouth, who were largely employed ferrying fish ashore from the anchored luggers, also went out to give aid when ships were in trouble, but the 'bargains' they struck made masters very reluctant to accept their help unless the situation was desperate. In a journal I have, dated 1816, recording a passage from Leith to London in a Berwick smack, the author writes of their conduct when a vessel in company touched on the Scroby sands. There was no immediate danger as the wind was light and tending to blow her off on the rising tide, but the two yawls which soon came alongside told the master his position was hopeless unless he availed himself of their assistance. The price demanded was more than the value of the ship and her cargo, but they hoped to get it because of the women on board, generally the beachmen's trump card. On this occasion, however, they were disappointed, the master standing by his judgment that she would re-float on her own, which she did within the hour, and continued on her way to London. The author concludes his account of this incident: 'I cannot mention the conduct of the boatmen of this place without feelings of strong indignation. They may be justly termed *harpies* which glut themselves with the sufferings of those who are miserable enough to encounter any misfortune on their coast.'

When mere survival was a bitter, relentless struggle, as in the years immediately after Waterloo, life was inevitably tough, crude and largely inhumane; there was little room for noble sentiments and in seeking to drive the hardest bargain they could the beach-men of Yarmouth, together with many more of their kind on every stretch of our coasts, were doubtless urged on by the need to provide food for hungry wives and children. But whatever may be placed on the debit side of their account a hundred and fifty years ago, it should be remembered on the credit side that within the next few decades as lifeboats became generally established, it was the longshoremen who formed their crews and laid the foundation of a service which is without equal anywhere in the world. They have, I think, long since wiped the slate clean and made ample amends for the transgressions of their forbears.

It seems an age, now, since my old friend Y.H.62. called out, 'Come on, young 'un, if yew've a mind t' go fishin',' but I do not regret being old enough to have known such men, to have made my 'first voyage' with them and to have been their companion, in good fortune and bad, when they were off using their skills to earn, what was at best, a precarious living. I learned many things from this self-imposed apprenticeship, the most important, per-haps, being respect at all times for the sea and the realisation that when out alone at night in a small boat, a measure of humbleness does not come amiss. That may not be exactly the right word but perhaps it explains why, as I throw out the first net, I invariably say, 'In the name of the Lord', and when I begin hauling in, 'Now for the Grand Secret'.

# Bibliography

Adams, W. M. *Popular History of Fisheries & Fishermen of all Countries.* 1883

Aflalo, F. G. *Sea Fishing Industry of England & Wales.* 1904

Bertram, J. G. *Harvest of the Sea.* 1865

—. *Unappreciated Fisher Folk.* 1883

Brabazon, W. *Deep Sea & Coast Fisheries of Ireland.* 1847

Buchanan-Wollaston, H. J. *Inshore Trawl Fisheries of Dorset & Devon.* 1933

Buckland, F. *Familiar History of British Fishes.* 1873

— and Walpole, S. *Report on the Sea Fisheries and Fishing Population of the United Kingdom.* 1883

Caux, J. W. de. *Herring & the Herring Fishery.* 1881

Chatterton, E. Keble. *King's Cutters & Smugglers.* 1912

Clark, R. *Black-Sailed Traders.* 1961

Collard, A. O. *Oyster & Dredgers of Whitstable.* 1902

Collins, Wilkie. *Rambles Beyond Railways.* 1851

Couch, J. *History of the Fishes of the British Islands.* 1878

Cruden, R. P. *History of Gravesend & the Port of London.* 1843

Davis, F. M. *Account of the Fishing Gear of England & Wales.* 1958

Dickens, Charles (fils). *Dictionary of the Thames.* 1892

Edinburgh, Duke of. *Notes on the Sea Fisheries & Fishing Population of the United Kingdom.* 1883

Fraser, R. *Review of the Domestic Fisheries of Great Britain & Ireland.* 1818

Holdsworth, E. W. H. *Deep-Sea Fishing & Fishing Boats.* 1874

Jusserand, J. J. *English Wayfaring Life in the Middle Ages.* 1899

Kristjonsson, H. (ed) *Modern Fishing Gear of the World.* 1965

Leslie, R. C. *Sea-Painter's Log.* 1886

— *Old Sea Wings, Ways & Words.* 1890

— *Waterbiography.* 1894

Mangin, A. *Mysteries of the Ocean.* 1870

Mayhew, H. *London Labour & the London Poor.* 1851

Moore, S. A. & H. S. *History & Law of Fisheries.* 1859

Murie, J. *Report on the Sea Fisheries of the Thames Estuary.* 1903

— Unpublished material in the Central Library, Scotland

Nall, J. G. *Chapters on the East Anglian Coast.* 1866

Patterson, A. H. *Nature in Eastern Norfolk.* 1905

Russell, W. Clark, and others. *British Seas.* 1894

Sawyer, F. E. *Sussex Fish & Fisheries.* 1882

Stacey-Watson, C. *Silvery Hosts of the North Sea.* 1883

Symonds, T. E. *Observations on the Fisheries of the West Coast of Ireland.* 1855

Tuer, A. W. *London Cries.* 1885

Washington, J. *Report on the Loss of Life & on the Damage Caused to Fishing Boats on the East Coast of Scotland in the Gale of 19 August, 1848.* 1849

White, A. *Popular History of British Crustacea.* 1857

White, P. *Observations upon the Present State of the Scotch Fisheries.* 1791

Wilcocks, J. C. *Sea-Fisherman.* 1875

Whymper, F. *Fisheries of the World.* 1883

Yarrell, W. *History of British Fishes.* 1859


*Douglas's Encyclopaedia.* c 1902

*Fishermen's Own Book.* Gloucester, Mass, 1882

*Penny Magazine.* 1837

# Index